IS MAN THE
PHOENIX?

TO
Robert and Alberta Reichenbach
who first taught me
about immortality,
and
C. S. Lewis
whose book *The Great
Divorce* made the
doctrine believable

IS MAN
THE PHOENIX?

A Study of Immortality

Bruce Reichenbach

UNIVERSITY
PRESS OF
AMERICA

Contents

Contents

The Phoenix

Amber splashed gold
orange tongues tinged yellow
the black bird of ancient lineage disappears
devoured by carnivorous white-hot flame.
Feathers float freely
hesitating, twisting
anticipating a final flutter.
Shudder.
Bone and sinew merge amid the acrid odor
in the cold grey ashes of the funeral pyre.

Rumor, whispered word
glimpsed beneath a cliff remotely placed
fledgling of speckled hue
singed wings stretched skyward
through swirling mist.
Real or spectral phantom?
Flesh or mocking spirit?
A distant rejuvenation born of conflagration?
Vestiges of semblance fire a myth
of Re-creation.

CHAPTER ONE

Life After Death: A Problem

"I BELIEVE IN . . . THE RESURRECTION OF THE BODY AND THE life everlasting." In this succinct manner the Apostles' Creed establishes belief in life after death as an essential component of the Christian faith. Though many beliefs in recent times have undergone significant decline in popularity among both laity and clergy, the belief in some kind of life after death is still widely held. Striking testimony is borne to this by the elaborate funeral arrangements which are initiated to preserve the corporeal remains of the deceased almost *ad infinitum*. The ancient practice of providing for the dead in the next life is continued, though not in precisely the same manner nor with the open avowal that this is what is being done in the mortuary ceremonies. The ancients supplied the deceased with food, liquids, eating utensils, and clothes so that he would not be deprived of these essentials either in his journey to the nether world or in the afterlife. Servants and such animals as dogs were buried with the corpse to provide the necessary service in the next life and guidance for the arduous journey to it. The Maya placed a jade bead in the mouth of the corpse, which it could barter for the keeping of its heart during a particularly hazardous section of the trip through the nine hells. The Egyptians supplied their royalty with a boat to traverse the dangerous waters of the underworld.

Though the accouterments today are different, the practice remains deeply embedded in our own mortuary rituals, a fact which reveals the conscious or subconscious belief in life after death. The corpse is embalmed and hermetically sealed in a metal casket to retard decay. It is surrounded with all sorts of comforts, such as plush satin lining and soft pillows; it is sent on its way, dressed in its finest clothes, accompanied by items cherished on earth — rings, family

1

pictures, even favorite pets. It is sacredly and silently interred in an expertly manicured setting, surrounded by gates, guards, and taboos.

Whereas these practices are most frequently accompanied by a faith in future divine activity, others show more of a willingness to entrust life after death to the progress of science. Some Americans are now beginning to explore ways of freezing the body and storing it in sealed containers. Upon death the body is cooled as rapidly as possible by the use of dry ice. When the danger of internal crystallization has passed, it is frozen at the temperature of liquid nitrogen, which terminates further biological disintegration. The hope is that biological science will advance to such an extent that in the future it will be able to restore this frozen body to life, and at the same time cure it of the ill which caused its death.

Man refuses to accept death as his end. There is a desire in many of us to be reunited with a close companion — parent, spouse, child, friend — who has died. That the relationships established with them are eternally severed seems unacceptable. Moreover, man in his finitude longs to escape the fearful finality of death; his preaching and practice reaffirm his faith that in the future God in his grace will grant, or science by its progress will procure, life after death.

But can we show good reason for maintaining such a belief? In light of what we now know about the composition of man and his physical and bodily processes, the extent of the universe, and the nature of physical structures and change, can we any longer reasonably maintain belief in the continuous and everlasting existence of the individual human being after death? Is this not a remnant myth from the prescientific age, crying out to be demythologized?

Cause for Concern

Every affirmation of belief in the existence of the individual human being after death encounters at least two significant facts, each of which poses difficult and serious problems for the believer in human immortality. The first is the fact of universal human mortality. Most of us choose to ignore death, particularly our own death; death is something that happens to somebody else. The automobile accident, cancer, heart attack, fire: these will not befall me. Yet, if we are honest with ourselves, we will discover that each of us is confronted with the reality and certainty of his own death. I remember only too well opening a Chicago newspaper and glancing at a photograph on the bottom of the page that caught my eye. Looking more closely I discovered that it was of a tombstone of a young man recently killed in combat in Vietnam. What struck me so forcefully was that his first name was the same as mine, as was his date of birth. That tombstone could have been mine; I could have been sent to the combat zone and been killed by a bullet or a land mine. I too was mortal, though I had not yet died as he had.

We too shall pass away. How, then, can we reconcile our belief in immortality with the hard fact of universal human mortality? How can we reasonably maintain that immortality (literally, not-dying) is not only a possibility but an actuality for every human being?

As if universal human mortality were not enough, this doctrine is also faced with the empirical fact of bodily corruption. Once the essential life functions cease, bodily disintegration begins, and that quickly. If the organic body, in most cases, is eventually destroyed and its atomic particles dispersed, what remains to be given life? What sense can be made of a resurrection where there is nothing to resurrect?

Indeed, if one speaks of resurrection as the raising of the same body, absurdities occur. For example, two individuals can share the same physical elements, for when the cannibal eats his enemy, the organic elements, which formerly constituted the body of his enemy, now serve to form his own body. Hence, in the resurrection, to paraphrase a Sadducean question, to whose body will it belong: the cannibal or his enemy?

If we would continue to believe in human immortality, these arguments to the contrary must be answered convincingly. For it must be admitted, I think, that the *prima facie* evidence is weighted in favor of the other side.

Why Worry About It?

But why, you may ask, should I be concerned to discuss the issue of life after death? This question can be asked from at least two perspectives. From the perspective of some who already maintain this belief, it means that they are not about to involve themselves in discussion of the intellectual presuppositions, arguments, and difficulties which lie behind or are inherent in their belief in immortality. They accept on faith the contention that there is life after death; nothing can shake them from that faith. Why should they question what they already know on the basis of faith?

What troubles me about this perspective is its view of faith. For such individuals, faith is a way of knowing; in particular, a way of knowing which operates from little or no evidence, requiring little or no evidence, sometimes affirming in the face of contrary evidence. It is a method which is often thought to be uniquely appropriate to religion, where objective and unambiguous evidence is so difficult to accumulate, where proofs seem to convince no one but their authors. Since the method of reason, applied to religion, appears to be nothing more than playing with language, faith must supplant reason. Consequently, to accept a certain dogma or proposition solely on the basis of faith is equivalent to saying that evidence is irrelevant to the determination of the truth or falsity of that belief.

Evidence might be thought irrelevant for several reasons. God as supernatural is considered to be beyond our human understanding. Our categories are derived from a finite world, yet God is infinite; our ideas represent the sensory world, yet God transcends sense experience. That "His ways are not our ways nor his thoughts our thoughts" implies that it is impossible to reason with human categories concerning the divine existence, nature, or program. Since human reason cannot penetrate to God, there can be no rational evidence which would confirm or falsify propositions about him, his nature, and his actions.

Others have contended that we cannot evaluate God's actions by the canons of our human logic. To bind God to our rules of correct thinking is to impose limits on that which is unlimited, to make that which is omnipotent less than all powerful. Others argue that since God has revealed himself to us in the Scriptures or the Church, we must accept what these say as authoritative without question. To reason concerning the authority and to require evidence for the pronouncements of that authority is to make reason the monarch and authority the subject. The crown of authority would rest on the head of reason.

The unfortunate consequence of this view of faith, however, is religious scepticism. If God is beyond human categories of thought, then there is nothing we can affirm meaningfully about him. If he is not subject to the laws of logic as manifested in his creation, we can draw no conclusions about him from our experience or concepts. We cannot make inferences or reason concerning his existence, his nature, his purposes, or his acts. Thus, we have no way of responding to those who claim that God does not exist or that he has different properties and characteristics from those which we believe by faith that he has. Without the use of human categories we cannot communicate about him or, since thought is so intrinsically bound up with language, think about him. Without evidence there is no good reason to believe in him, to trust in him over another god, or even to move from unbelief to belief. Without concepts to apply or the ability to make inferences we must be, at best, sceptical about God.

Similarly with authority. If we accept certain documents or institutions or individuals to be authoritative on the basis of faith, requiring no evidence, we have no grounds on which to recommend our particular authority. Why should anyone else accept and adopt my chosen authority rather than another's? Why should the Christian Scriptures be more authoritative than the Koran or the Book of Mormon or the Hindu Vedas? Why are the Apostles more authoritative than the Greek philosophers or Moslem sufis or Hindu gurus? Without evidence, we are left to the uncertain call of the trumpet; we have no criteria to enable us to choose to whose banner to rally, in whose army to serve.

Evidence must be relevant to our beliefs, if we are to find the truth, discourse intelligently about it, and attempt to convince others likewise to believe what we conceive to be true. Faith without evidence lacks the rational basis needed to make a decision about the content and object of that faith, or to help us distinguish between conflicting claims. We must set out and evaluate the evidence, pro and con, that in this case affects the doctrine of human immortality.

The second perspective is a kind of intellectual fatalism. *Que sera, sera* — what will be, will be. We cannot *know* about the future, about what will or will not occur. Discourse about the future can be nothing other than speculation. Only after we are dead will we have any evidence or knowledge of whether or not immortality is a fact. Why should we be concerned with exploring the issue now? We must live and deal with that which affects the present. If life after death is a reality, it will occur whether or not we think about it; if not, no amount of theologizing or philosophizing will bring it to pass. If there is immortality, we will obtain certain knowledge of it at that time; if not, it hardly matters, since we will not be there to discern its non-occurrence.

Though this position might appear initially attractive, its logical implication is intellectual suicide. With perhaps the exception of the existence of my present acts of thinking, there is nothing of experience which can be known with certainty — past, present, or future. That Benjamin Franklin was an ambassador to France *could* be an historical error; that a grey, four-drawer filing cabinet now stands in the corner of this room *could* be the product of an hallucination or the component of a dream. These apparent facts have a high degree of probability, but not certainty. But the absence of certitude does not affect our belief that these are really facts about the past and the present. We hold them to be items of knowledge because they are well-justified true beliefs. And if lack of certitude does not cause us to relinquish the intellectual search for knowledge about past or present, it should not do so regarding the future. If we abandon inquiry into questions about the future on the grounds that they cannot be answered with certainty, we must abandon investigation into questions about the present as well. Hence, either we totally forsake the intellectual quest for knowledge, or we press on to discover well-justified true beliefs about the past, present, *and* future, demanding and evaluating evidence and reasoning. Rather than resign from investigating about the future, we must research that much harder to discover what can and what cannot be said about future states of affairs, about what is possible and what is not possible, about what is reasonable to expect and can be stated meaningfully and what is nonsense.

Moreover, contrary to the objection developed from this perspective, the future does bear on the present. It is to the credit of the Existentialists that they have unswervingly asserted that I am my projects, that how I view the future influences my present choices and course of action. The future becomes part of the present as it informs how I live in the face of what is to come. With regard to immortality, the doctrine concerns both my present moral conduct and the manner in which I live as a being-unto-death.

Traditionally, the belief in immortality has been associated with recommendations to moral action, insofar as reward and punishment were considered to constitute either part of or a sanction of an adequate ethical principle. As the seventeenth-century philosopher John Locke noted, all laws need sanctions or enforcers, for without them there is no encouragement or compulsion to do the good. Reward and punishment act as reinforcers or enforcers of the moral law and are therefore essential parts of the moral law. Even if one does not follow Locke by not including reward and punishment within the ethical principle itself, there is little doubt that rewards serve to reinforce and encourage the continuance of prescribed actions, whereas punishments (perhaps less successfully) act as deterrents. Christian theology contends that divine judgment will be administered to all in the afterlife. God will reward the good and punish the evil. If such be the case, the reality of immortality and its accompanying divine judgment can affect ethical performance here and now. Knowing that God will eternally reward good should encourage right action; correspondingly, knowing the severity of his punishment of evil should function as a deterrent to evil action. Thus, the doctrine of immortality, when viewed from this theistic perspective, can have an impact on present conduct as a sanction of the moral law.

Secondly, belief in immortality bears upon the way in which I live in the face of death. Is death the end of my existence? What really ceases to exist? Will I — as the real person — die? Answers to these questions will affect the way in which I view my own death. My death, your death, is imminent. Viewed from the total span of human existence on this earth, our individual stay is extremely brief: a minute as compared to a year. How will you face death? Will you fight it as the terminus of existence? Will you see it as a necessary stage preparatory to another existence? Will you accept it in hope, in resolute affirmation of its finality, or in resignation? What are you doing now in anticipation of your death? Are you preparing for an ending or a beginning? The answers, in part, depend upon how you respond to the question of the actuality of life after death. How you live now does depend on your view of the future.

Hence, we must not abdicate from the responsibility to evaluate the evidence with respect to the doctrine of immortality. We must search for the belief which is best justified by evidence.

Where Do We Go From Here?

Granted, then, that our quest is meaningful and significant, where do we go from here?

The difficulties already pointed out indicate that more is involved in a consideration of the problem of human immortality than merely the obvious question, "Is man immortal?" Indeed, the usual objections to human immortality rarely are raised against arguments which purport to prove it. Rather, as evidenced in this chapter, the objections originate from an analysis of the nature of man and the human organism. Almost without exception, the denial of human immortality is supported by the contention that the nature of man is such that he cannot be immortal. Even if one could per chance present convincing reasons for a state of post-mortem existence, or describe in meaningful language such a condition of existence, the argument goes, man is such a being that his death and bodily destruction make it impossible for him to ever partake of this state of existence. It does not make sense to say that he can survive his death. Accordingly, the above-stated question really presupposes a prior query, "Is immortality possible for man?" If there are no conditions under which man is capable of living after his death, then one need not bother to ask the first question. Only when a positive answer can be given to the second query does the first question become important; further arguments then are needed to establish that the possibility of life after death will be actualized.

Therefore, we have two questions before us. First, "What must man be like in order for there to be the possibility that he could live subsequent to his death?" and second, "What good reasons can be given for maintaining a belief in life after death?" Chapters three through six will be devoted to the first question, while in chapters seven and eight we will consider the second question by discussing reasons for believing in the actuality of human immortality. Finally, in chapter nine we will pose some intriguing questions about what one can meaningfully say about the manner of immortal existence.

CHAPTER TWO

What Does "Immortality" Mean?

THE DISCUSSION OF IMMORTALITY FREQUENTLY COMMENCES in a cloud of ambiguity, for those who address themselves to the problem of human immortality understand the term in several different ways. This is particularly the case in the twentieth century, when the grip which traditional Christian dogmas have held on Western theological thought has been significantly loosened. In this chapter I intend to present four different interpretations of "immortality," and ultimately to opt for the last as the one to inform our future discussion.

Immortality as Remembrance

One commonly held view states that immortality is realized in the living presence of oneself in the things, persons, or events which continue after one is deceased. In the act of creation the artisan endows the created object with a part of himself. The cabinet maker takes more than mere pride in his hand-crafted woodwork; part of himself endures in that carefully wrought creation. Its form and shape are his brainchild; in the long hours of cutting, forming, and smoothing, his hands have molded themselves into the fine-grained wood. Since he is in that creation, injury can be inflicted on him by mistreatment of his creation. Carelessness toward, mishandling, or lack of proper appreciation of the object is an affront to the artisan himself. Since he is part of that object and because he knows that it will endure long after he has died, he too can survive his own death. He will be remembered for that cabinet: made by＿＿＿＿.

Likewise the writer or the artist puts something of his own soul or self into his creation. Through that which he gives it of himself, he attempts to communicate to others his beliefs, hopes, fears, despairs, and troubles; the medium is used to describe his view of the world and human experience. Thus one can look at an oil painting or read a literary work, and thereby understand something of the author, and, in that understanding, bring the creator of the work back into existence. He lives again under the watchful eye of another; he is re-created every time his painting is viewed or his prose read. The artist believes or hopes that his creation has a lasting significance, such that its fame or renown or communicative ability will continue long after his own death. In effect, immortality for the writer or artist comes about through the continuing presence of himself, his ideas, ideals, perspectives, and abilities, in his lasting creations.

Immortality in the sense of remembrance can likewise be gained through the painting of one's acts on the canvas of history. By holding political office, by winning or losing battles, by revolting against authority or the status quo, by committing outrageous crimes, by making great discoveries, men have gained fame and renown; their name and the memory of their deeds long survive them. Their decisions and actions have forever altered the course of the world, such that what comes after them could not have occurred without them, nor have been other than it was because of them. In this sense, Adolf Hitler has achieved immortality; his name, his presence, the consequences of his decisions and actions will live on, presently in infamy, perhaps later (recalling the so-called great personages of history — Alexander, Caesar, Napoleon) as a famous and great leader to be studied, written about, and discussed. In any case, he will never be forgotten, nor can the way he altered the geography of Europe and the course of world history be ignored.

Others find their immortality in the lives of other people whom they have affected. If they have helped to change someone for the good, if the quality of life of another is improved because of who they were and what they did, they will live on in that person. They will be remembered.

The American philosopher George Santayana has suggested that the human need for immortality and the frustration of knowing that one's own being is mortal find their outlet in human reproduction.[1] In the offspring, a counterfeit of one's self is given life, to survive after one's own death. One is assured that one's name, lineage, ideas, and ideals will be passed on to the future through one's children. Consequently, one can explain the desire to have male children which will continue the family name, and the parental pressure on the children to believe what the parents believe, to think as they do, to espouse the same ideals and values. Children are the promise and grandchildren the assurance of a vicarious immortality.

All of these views have one crucial element in common: human memory. One's own immortality is entrusted to the memory of others; one creates, acts, decides, procreates — all in order to be remembered. One survives his death when another remembers him. Hence, one may define "immortality" in this first sense as "the lasting memory which others will have of one's self, because of the deeds one has performed."

An interesting and important feature of this view of immortality is that it clearly relates to the question of the source of meaning in a person's existence, for that by which one creates a remembrance of one's self is very likely that by which one discovers or creates meaning for one's own existence. If, for example, one finds meaning and fulfillment in the activity of writing, and if one does it well so that what is written endures, at the same time that one is creating meaning for oneself by the written page, one is producing the means for one's own immortality. Or again, many individuals find the meaning for their lives in their children. Long hours are spent playing with them and reading to them; many of the finer things in life are forgone in order to give them the clothes or education or cars that they need or want. This time and sacrifice are not regretted; they are activities which give meaning and purpose to the lives of the parents, for they have centered their lives and everything that they do around their children. The offspring are their source of meaning and purpose for existence. Thus, contemporary with their discovery of real meaning for their lives, in their children the parents have created and are preserving that which will give them (vicarious) immortality.

Though this view of immortality is helpful in relating immortality to the attainment of meaning in life, it fails to touch the heart of the issue with which we are concerned. In particular, it does not seem to be a distinctively moral or religious definition of the term. As we noted in the first chapter, the religious view of immortality is usually associated with that which encourages or reinforces moral action and discourages or provides sanctions against immoral action. Insofar as immortality is made possible by or related to a God who rewards and

11

punishes, it is looked upon as an incentive for earthly moral living. But immortality as remembrance, rather than encouraging performance of the good, only advises the accomplishment of *noteworthy* things. The moral quality of that consequence is left open; what matters is whether it is memorable. Unfortunately, the stress solely on memorability encourages, if anything, evil rather than good. That which yields memorability is the remarkableness of the consequences of the action performed. But immoral acts — as in the case of those of Adolf Hitler, Al Capone, Richard Nixon, or G. Gordon Liddy — are often more likely to gain one immortality in this sense than moral actions. The crime gains access to the mass media, and the criminal thereby gains renown. It is the act of destruction which is frequently recorded, rarely the act of construction. Though this is not always the case — witness Jesus and Luther, Confucius and Gandhi, Bach and Picasso — the fact that it is often the case, and more importantly that this view fails to lead to the recommendation of good over evil, suggests that this cannot be acclaimed a religious view of immortality.

Secondly, though immortality as remembrance poses problems for the one who seeks to attain to it, the problems posed are of a practical rather than a theoretical nature. That I will be remembered is uncertain; there is no way to guarantee it. Indeed, for most individuals immortality as remembrance is doomed to failure, for only a very select few escape the fate of being remembered for no more than a brief and fleeting moment. Most individuals are ultimately forgotten; their names, if ever recorded at all, are lost in the dusty pages of newspapers, books, hospital records, and obituary columns. Only an infinitesimal fraction of the three and one-half billion people alive today will be remembered past the third or fourth generation, if that long. Hence, the human need for immortality is destined to unfulfillment; the hope for remembrance is overshadowed by the almost certain forgetfulness of future generations. Moreover, those few who are remembered are rarely remembered as more than a name, or as they really were or would have liked to be remembered. The historical personage is most often misunderstood; why else the continual need for "reinterpretations" of the lives of the great. And this, too, is tragic, for as Albert Camus points out, from the blackness of the earth one cannot correct the misconceptions of one's deeds, ideas, or creations. Thus, if immortality is interpreted in this sense, it is, almost from its inception, doomed to be unrealized, and certainly unrealized in the sense the individual intended.

The problem posed here is a *practical* one; that is, what can I do to ensure not only that *I* will be one of those whose remembrance endures, but also that my legacy will be correctly understood? But the problems posed in chapter one are different: can man be immortal, and what evidence is there that he is? It is not the practical issue concerning the manner of achieving immortality which compelled our initial consideration, but the theoretical issues whether there be any such state of affairs and whether man, in view of what he is, can attain it. Thus, though one may surely define "immortality" as "remembrance," it should be made clear that this definition has practical, not theoretical, issues in view. That is, when so defined the reader should understand that the subject under consideration is *how* to attain lasting renown and memorability.

Immortality as a Way of Life

Recently some thinkers have suggested that the immortality of the soul has nothing to do with a life that extends beyond or begins after death. Death is not an event that a person experiences, like drinking coffee or getting chicken pox. One can be aware of sipping hot coffee, or the insatiable itching of the chicken pox, but one cannot be aware of one's own death.[2] It does not make sense to say that one can witness one's own death, for this implies that I am both a living witness and a dead object which is witnessed. This is patently contradictory: one cannot be both alive and dead simultaneously. Thus, death is different from all other of my experiences; indeed, it is not an experience at all, but the termination of my experience. It is an event for spectators, not for participants.

Moreover, as the end of all my possibilities, death likewise differs from other experiences in that it is nonsense to say it can be survived. It makes sense to say that I can survive my heart attack or that the canoeist survived the dangerous journey through the boiling rapids. But if death is the end of all experience, it hardly makes sense to say that one can survive one's own death. For example, the statement "He was killed in the plane crash in New Delhi, but he survived" is *prima facie* absurd.

Accordingly, it is necessary to reinterpret "immortality" in terms of our present experience and life.[3] Consider, first of all, the statement, "Man has a soul." If one takes this statement to be akin to the statement, "Man has a heart," impossible questions follow: Will you show it to me? Where is it? How does it contact and influence the body? Language about the soul as an entity or substance must be seen in its true light to be language about the kind of life one is living. For example, the statement, "He sold his soul to the devil," is not to be understood as a mercantile transaction between the individual and the devil, where the individual literally gives up a part of himself in exchange for some quantity of goods or services. It is not like selling one's old suit of clothing to the second-hand store. Rather, this statement indicates that the person intends to lead a life of self-gratification, a life not characterized by pursuit of moral virtues. He is willing to abandon his moral principles at the first opportunity for personal material gain. Similarly, the rhetorical question in the Bible, "What does it profit a man if he gain the whole world and lose his own soul?" does not speak about a bargain one might strike up, where one swaps a part of himself called the soul for profits or pleasures or, indeed, the entire world. Nor is it referring to an object lost but possibly found by the diligent searcher. Rather, it indicates that a life of material good fortune which is not accompanied by the highest moral and religious standards is ultimately a life not well-lived. Thus, statements about the state of a man's soul are assertions about the kind of life he is living and the moral and religious reflections he makes on that life.

Similarly, eternal life is not to be looked upon as an extension of one's life, as an appendage to present earthly existence. Rather, it is the reality of goodness; it is that in terms of which human life is to be assessed. Eternity is not *more* life, but *quality* of life.

> The difference between the man who aspired to eternal life in this sense and a man who did not would not be the difference between a man who did think he would live on after death and a man who did not think that he would live on after death. The difference would show in the attitudes they had to their respective lives. In one man, his desires and appetites would be, or would be aimed at being, subordinate to moral considerations, while in the other they would reign unchecked.[4]

Thus, when religion speaks about the eternal life of the soul, it indicates that what is important is the overcoming of death. Not in the sense that one survives his death, or manages to live on indefinitely, but in the sense of dying to oneself. The eternal life of the soul is the moral quality of life which characterizes one's earthly existence here and now. To strive for eternal life is to seek to live unselfishly, dying to oneself for the love of others. "I am suggesting, then, that eternal life for the believer is participation in the life of God, and that this life has to do with dying to the self, seeing that all things are a gift from God, that nothing is ours by right or necessity."[5]

What can be said about this definition of immortality? First, it appears that this view has confused two very different dimensions of human existence. Existence has, indeed, a qualitative sense about it. Concern can be manifested for the quality of life, both in the sense of the physical and social environment in which one lives and works, and in the sense of the kind of life one leads in that world, that is, concern for the moral and spiritual values which are realized through interaction with others. But existence has a quantitative aspect as well. The insurance company is financially interested in the length of time one lives; we speak about so-and-so's untimely death; we celebrate so-and-so's 100th birthday with the question, "What is your secret for long life?" However, those who hold this view of immortality want to dissolve the second dimension of life into the first. It is true that the doctrine of immortality has implications for the quality of life here and now, for the way in which I choose to live. But to say that it has such *implications* is not to say that that is what such a doctrine *means*. Similarly with the notion of eternal life. If I believe that there exists a God who is concerned with my own existence, spiritual condition, and the moral and religious acts which I perform here and now, such that the state and quality of my future existence depends on this, then the notion of eternal life does have implications for the quality of my life here and now. But again, to say that the concept of eternal life has such implications is not to say that that is what this concept *means*. "Eternal" is a temporal notion, such that one cannot use this term apart from a concern with time. Thus, though this definition is helpful in that it focuses attention on the moral and religious implications which this doctrine has for our present life, as an explanation of what immortality means it is found wanting.

Secondly, this doctrine of immortality leaves the historical question untouched. I still want to know about what will happen to me, if anything, after my death. Is death the terminus of my existence? Should I prepare myself for a life which would begin after my death? If death is the end, in what respect does what I do now have any importance or lasting significance? This definition of immortality leaves these questions not only unanswered, but untreated.

Finally, this view of immortality rescues the very significant moral import of the doctrine, which was absent from the first definition proposed, but at the price of conflicting with the ordinary view of eternal life. According to the common interpretation, immortality is a doctrine which concerns the period of time subsequent to the individual's death; here the emphasis is on the present. However, disagreement with or departure from the ordinary view does not mean that the new interpretation is wrong. Indeed, it might well be the case that the common view is in need of correction or alteration. A reinterpretation would be a helpful and necessary contribution if it could be shown that there is no good reason to maintain or good reason not to maintain the ordinary view.

In fact, this very claim forms one of the foundations on which this re-interpretation is constructed. Those who propose this definition contend that the traditional definition of immortality is meaningless. Death is not an event which one can experience, nor which one can survive. It does not even make sense to speak about surviving one's own death. But this contention, I think, can be disputed. Indeed, the following chapters will concentrate precisely on this point by analyzing and evaluating what sense can be made of the doctrine that man can live subsequent to his own death. Hence, final evaluation of this re-interpretation must await judgment on the success of our presentation.

Immortality as Reunion With the One

A third analysis of immortality is given by those who maintain that everything in the universe is ultimately one. Each thing has its source not in something which is completely distinct from itself, not as originating out of nothing (*ex nihilo*), but as coming from the very being of that which is ultimately real. There is but one fundamental reality, though it is called by various names: Absolute, Being, God, *Brahman*, or *Tao*. Though each particular thing might be temporarily separate from the Source of its existence, it is never completely separate. Through appropriate action here on earth, that which is finite can be reunited with its Source of existence. This reunification is not like that of a son with his family, but is the actual union with the One.

This theme is present in both Western and non-Western

philosophies. According to Chinese Taoism (in its more philosophical forms) everything that exists in the universe is part of the whole or *Tao*. Indeed, there really exists only one thing, Nature or *Tao*. It is the totality of all things, both as the transcendent Unity and the myriad manifestations which are born of *Tao*. Everything arises out of it, asserts itself in its separateness, and in the end is once more merged into the whole.

Man is unique in that he can understand something about *Tao* itself, as well as the necessity for everything to return to *Tao*. He can recognize the unity of the cosmic process, and make unity with all things his goal. He can "relax in the realm of the infinite and thus abide in the realm of the infinite."[6] Moreover, he can accelerate the process of return to *Tao* and experience unity with all things by abandoning his self-seeking passion and by cultivating his *Ti*, his natural, instinctive, primitive qualities or virtues. Man therefore gains immortality in the conscious acceptance and identification with *Tao* here on earth and his final union with *Tao*. The life achieved is not a separate existence; indeed, separateness and distinction are the source of the difficulties which constitute the human predicament. Rather, immortality comes through union with *Tao*, of which all things are manifestations.

A similar theme is present in the *Upanishads*, which form part of the sacred writings of the Hindus.[7] Reality is ultimately one, though it can be viewed either from the perspective of subject or self (*ātman*) or from the perspective of object or the reality which evolves itself as this world (*Brahman*). The individual self which I am (*ātman*) transcends my senses, mind, intellect, feeling, and will; my essence or soul is pure knowledge, pure consciousness. But my consciousness is not independent of all other consciousness; rather, in my own self cosmic or universal consciousness is manifested. Since *ātman* is *Brahman*, my individual consciousness is a manifestation or appearance of the whole, the One.

Human existence is characterized by *samsāra*, which is the cyclical process of evolution from the One (*Brahman*) and resolution back into it. Man forgets his essential unity or identity with *Brahman*; he believes that he is finite and distinct from it, and asserts his self-identity at the price of failure to live in harmony with the world. Thus, he enters into *samsāra*. For each individual soul this means thousands of reincarnations in lives punctuated by suffering. Caught

17

in the cycle of suffering, man's goal becomes freedom or *moksha:* release from the cycle of reincarnations. This is achieved by the cultivation of detachment and by right knowledge, in particular, realization of the unity of everything as *Brahman.* When *moksha* is obtained, one has true immortality; the individual *ātman* is one with the whole, reabsorbed into the universal consciousness of the One. This final union occurs either just before death, or at death. Reincarnations cease; individuality no longer obtains. My *ātman* is one with *Brahman.*

In the West this analysis of immortality has been given a more existential turn by the distinguished theologian, Paul Tillich. All men, he contends, are sinners; that is, they are separated from other men, from their own selves, and ultimately from the Ground of their being, God. Sin is thus the state of separation in which they find themselves. But God gives grace to all men. Grace is the reunion of my life with that of those around me, the reconciliation of my self with itself, and the acceptance into and reunion with the origin or source of my own life, God. We are bound to the Ground of our being for all eternity; we can never escape God. Thus, all men will experience, through God's grace, eternal life or immortality.

However, he is careful to point out that such terms as "immortality" and "Eternal Life" are not descriptive concepts to be taken literally; they do not indicate an empirical or historical event. "Immortality" is not an extension of life which a spiritual soul will experience at some future time subsequent to an historical death. It does not describe the manner of future existence of a separately existing soul. Neither does "eternal" describe a length of time during which such a disembodied soul might exist. Eternity is not a matter of quantity of time.

Rather, these theological terms are symbols, and as symbols, one must search for their existential meaning, that is, for what they have to say to my own present existence, the problems and evils which I daily face within my world, and the saving relationships which overcome my separation. Symbols point beyond themselves, but they are not literally descriptive of that reality to which they point. If they are taken literally, absurdities and contradictions result; we are forced into irreconcilable paradoxes. Neither are symbols empirically grounded or refutable by experience. Rather, they open up the levels of reality which are to be encountered in religious experience. These levels of reality, which exist both outside and within us, constitute the foundation for the relationship between God and man in the Christian experience.

What, then, is the meaning of the symbol "immortality" (or "Eternal Life," since for him immortality is merely a negative way of saying eternal life)? Tillich notes that it symbolizes two things. First, it symbolizes the fulfillment or, as he terms it, the essentialization, of our own being. We find ourselves caught up in finite human existence, threatened by such negative things as illness, evil, death, and destruction. In the face of this threat, we seek to discover and realize our own potential, to find fulfillment, meaning, and purpose for our lives. Eternal life symbolizes the discovery of such fulfillment, to the extent that by my decisions and actions I realize my destiny; I am transformed by God to become what I was destined to become, however imperfectly accomplished. This is an event that is not projected for the future but occurs in the present. Thus, the promise of eternal life means that I will find meaning and personal fulfillment, that my total personality will be spiritually transformed, and that I will overcome the negatives which threaten me: in this life I will become a "New Being."[8]

Secondly, "Eternal Life" symbolizes the relation of the temporal to the eternal, or better, the transition of finite human existence into the eternal. Since each individual is created a finite creature out of the eternal Ground of being, each is rooted in eternity, in the eternal God. Hence, the individual will return in immortality to the eternal from which it comes. This is not a future act in history, but rather discloses our present participation in the Ground of being, insofar as we are accepted in grace and are reunited with him from whom we are estranged. It symbolizes our ultimate oneness with God, in whom we realize our true being.[9]

This return occurs for every existent being. No finite being can be understood in isolation from other beings or persons; to understand oneself fully one must understand the relations which I have with others and with my world. The source of the unity of everything is the universal derivation of all things from God. Hence, the doctrine of the unity of everything in divine love means that all beings will return to that unity, to God.[10] Love overcomes death. No being can exist apart from or independent of that unity, nor can any finite being fail to attain participation in the eternal, though when threatened by the negatives of illness, despair, or death we sometimes fear that we will not attain to eternal life. But ultimately we cannot cease to exist (participate in non-being), because then the unity of all Being would be destroyed. Eternal life and immortality thus mean that we can, indeed, will, participate in the being of God.

What, then, of my own self-conscious identity; do I continue to be aware of myself when I am unified with God? Tillich gives a not unambiguous answer. He asserts that we must affirm two apparently contradictory, negative statements. On the one hand, the "self-conscious self cannot be excluded from Eternal Life,"[11] for the finite being cannot participate in the life of the eternal unless there is another of which it can be aware. Life involves interaction and hence difference between the participants in life. Therefore the individual self cannot be excluded from eternal life. On the other hand, the body does not continue to exist, either in its old form or in a new form; neither does the self continue on, aware of itself, with a memory of past events. Thus, "the self-conscious self in Eternal Life is not what it is in temporal life." In short, the self will continue on, but in another form, about which Tillich cannot tell us, since to do so, he assures us, he would have to lapse into poetry. This answer is consistent with his claim that to take the symbols literally results in contradiction.

In summary, Tillich contends that all is one, that everything is ultimately part of Being-itself (God). But in becoming a finite being, man has become separated from God; disconnectedness (sin) characterizes his relations with the world and with himself. The doctrine of universal salvation, however, holds that all men will be saved, that nothing will ever be lost from God into what Tillich calls non-being. Hence, all men experience immortality, the reunion with God. This reunion is not an historical event experienced by a separated soul. Rather, the meaning of immortality is that each person will ultimately realize his own unique being in becoming a New Being, and that his separateness from God will be overcome in being united with his Ground or Source of being.

Critique

This notion of immortality as reunion with the One seems defective for several reasons. First, this view appears to be singularly uninteresting, at least to the individual who is supposed to be immortal. In being unified with the One, I lose my individuality and self-consciousness. Though I gain immortality, I do not know it, neither has it any continuing personal fulfillment for me. In effect, I never realize for myself this immortality. I merely become part of the whole or One: *Brahman, Tao,* or Ground of being.

The response of Hinduism is that this objection is both mistaken and insignificant. It is mistaken because the liberation which the individual experiences from *samsāra* has personal significance for the individual. His suffering is ended; no more will he become incarnate and subject to the painful vicissitudes of existence.

It is insignificant because the self as a distinct, self-conscious entity is not ultimately important. Indeed, the human predicament is traced to man's concern with the self, to his affirmation of the discreteness of his finite self, and to his failure to recognize his unity with the whole. Evil is not due to an offense against the gods, nor does it result from refusal to sacrifice to them or from improper conduct of worship. Evil is the metaphysical error of distorting ultimate reality by dividing it into parts and treating those parts as distinct from each other. The consequence of this evil is a world in disharmony. Each man, viewing himself as distinct from all others, seeks to aggrandize himself and promote his own interests. Accordingly, if all evil originates in *ahamkāra* — the affirmation of the finite self — it is absurd to preserve that which is the source of evil. Disunity and human suffering will be eliminated only when each realizes that he is not a separate being and ends the promotion of his own self. A doctrine of immortality which provides for the continued existence of the conscious individual would only serve to increase the evil in the world. When it is realized that the true source of evil is *ahamkāra,* the objection loses its importance.

One's evaluation of this reply depends ultimately upon one's view of the nature of reality and of the human predicament. We shall have something to say about the metaphysic involved shortly; here just a few words about the Hindu view of the nature of the human condition are in order. Hinduism views the human predicament as originating from false beliefs about the nature of reality, not as having to do with any relation to a divine being. The consequences of maintaining false beliefs are disharmony and evil acts performed against others. Salvation comes through knowledge, through the realization of the true nature of the self and its relation to the whole. As such, Hinduism presupposes that man, from within himself and by his own abilities and powers, can accomplish the liberation required by the severity of the human predicament. But can man save himself? Personally, I cannot see how this is possible. History bears witness to man's continued failure to achieve good by himself. Humanistic efforts at creating a perfect moral and social order have inevitably been unsuccessful. Good intentions never seem sufficient: what I realize I should do I find myself not doing, and conversely, what I realize I should not do I do. Unless man be provided with a power from without, his efforts are destroyed by his own self-seeking nature. Man cannot liberate himself; only God as an agent external to man can do that.

However, our objection presupposes that reality is plural. Thus, even here in our discussion of the nature of the human predicament, we are forced back to evaluating conflicting views of reality. If reality is one, evil is affirmation of distinctness; if reality is plural, evil consists in severed relationships and their consequences. If reality is one, there can be no question of aid from an external agent; if reality is plural, external agents can provide the needed power of liberation. If our argument in the previous paragraph is correct, man's need of external aid points to a reality which is plural. But a final decision as to which is the correct view awaits a determination of the metaphysical issue.

Tillich's response to the critic's suggestion is to deny that this interpretation of immortality is insignificant to me as an individual. Its significance is found in the promise that in this present life I will attain fulfillment of my true self. I find this fulfillment when I become a New Being; then my being becomes essence. And what could be more significant for me than to realize my being. But what about the paradoxical pair of statements that I do not lose my finite self-consciousness or individuality, but neither do I retain it? What does this mean? It means that it is *I* who become a New Being; the sin which separated *me* from other beings and from the Ground of being is removed. It also means that by becoming a New Being, my *separation* from God and from other beings will be overcome. Immortality promises a full restoration of my being to its true place of union with others and with the Ground of being.

Yet, I think the objection remains in part, for Tillich also wants to indicate the objective condition of the human individual. If the separation existing between my being and the Ground of being is removed and I become one with Being-itself, the impossibility of my recognizing this new situation is created by the absence of a true subject-object dichotomy. I cannot appreciate my new (or renewed) status, though now as a separate being I can be reassured that this will be my fulfillment and can foretaste what existential meaning this status would have through recognition of the significance of the symbols employed. Tillich's view of the function of symbols prevents him from clarifying the objective status of the individual in relation to the Ground of being.

Secondly, the moral implications of this view of immortality are either purely negative or else seemingly non-existent. For Hinduism, which holds that reunion occurs after numerous incarnations, the moral import of the doctrine of immortality is purely negative. Progress in moral living is sought in order to attain *moksha*, that is, release from the sufferings of seemingly endless reincarnations. Salvation is an *escape* from something, not a movement toward any positive state. Indeed, the ethic which evolves from this is an ethic predominantly of knowledge, not of action. *Moksha* comes through right knowledge (that *ātman* is *Brahman*, that all is one) accompanied or preceded by the cultivation of detachment, i.e., the eradication of the selfish impulses which are a result of viewing the self as distinct. Liberation from *samsāra* does not come through right action (though this was rectified in the later *Bhagavad-Gita*).

For others, who like Tillich assert universal salvation or the assurance of reunion with God, there seem to be no moral implications for my existence at all. It appears that no matter what I do or how I act, I am assured that I will be reunited with the Ground of being.

Tillich denies this, stating that the threat of eternal death counter-balances the assurances of eternal life. Here again he poses two contradictory statements to create existential understanding: man faces the threat of eternal death or non-being; man has the assurance that love conquers death and that all will be saved. But in the end, Tillich affirms that no one can fail to attain eternal life, for this would mean that that which once was being now is non-being. This would accomplish the impossible: the destruction of the unity of being. Thus, anyone who truly understands Tillich's position cannot help but be assured that he will achieve eternal life; the threat of eternal death and non-being is overcome, not by moral action, but by *under-*

standing that death or non-being is not real.

Tillich might respond that we have only focused on the second of the two meanings of "Eternal Life." We have forgotten the first, which stresses that eternal life is the fulfillment of our unique potential. Our fulfillment or essentialization would certainly include moral progress, though not moral perfection. Self-realization will be not complete, but a matter of degree. [12] But if we are assured of reunion with Being-itself, need we even claim that self-fulfillment or essentialization must occur at all for there to be immortality? Will the unfulfilled or, since Tillich denies there is any such being, the one who has achieved the least amount of fulfillment, gain immortality? With his thesis of the unity of being, it would appear that he would have to reply in the affirmative. Thus, moral advance is not a prerequisite for eternal life, or even implied by it.

Thirdly, as we have already indicated, acceptance of this definition of immortality depends, in large part, upon the adoption of a particular metaphysic or view of reality. For those who hold this view, reality is ultimately one; everything is either a manifestation or an appearance of the One. As an *appearance,* each object is like the side of a coin. The penny shows itself as "heads" when Lincoln's face appears; "tails" when his memorial is up. But though there are two sides, one does not possess two cents. Each side is an appearance of the one penny. As a *manifestation,* each particular is like a drop of water. In diverse containers each drop is separate from the others, but when poured together, they form one large drop; the many are multiple manifestations of the one drop.

This view of reality entails that there is ultimately no difference between particular individuals or things. They may appear to be different or manifest themselves as distinct entities, but to think that they really or ultimately are distinct is a mistake. God is ultimately not different from the world; the world and everything in it either comes out of him and returns to him or is an appearance of him.

The crucial difficulty which faces this view of reality is whether it can adequately account for our human experience of the diversity of beings in the world. According to the view that everything is merely an *appearance* of the One, diversity and plurality are illusions. The One is the real; plurality is an illusory appearance. But is the world of plurality simply illusion? Is the difference between you and me or the difference between you and an inanimate object merely an apparent one? Is it a mistake to think that there is a *real* difference between things? To the contrary, human experience seems to confirm the reality of plurality in the world and the distinctiveness of the things which it contains. We occupy distinct places, indicating the reality of spatial relations between discrete objects. We think unique, personal, private thoughts, pointing to the discreteness of individual consciousness. We exist at different times, from which we infer the reality of temporal relations. Rather than diversity constituting a mistaken and illusory view of the world, it would seem that the position which denies diversity is mistaken.

According to the view that everything is a *manifestation* of the One, there must be some principle which accounts for the diversity which comes out of the One. But what is it about the One which causes or encourages it to become many? If it is perfect and complete in itself, what need has it to become multiple or diverse? If it is essentially consciousness, and hence intrinsically aware of itself as constituting reality, it would seem to know what would be the fruits of diversity. Diversity brings forth evil, illusion, separation and its resulting inhumanity between men, and fear and despair at impending death and destruction. If it knows this, why does it become diverse?

The answer might be given that it does not allow or will diversity, but that this is a natural result of the activity of the principle of diversity. But what is the status of this principle? Is it part of the One or is it separate from it? If the latter, we have two principles — the One as the principle of unity, and a separate principle of diversity. But this dualism cannot be consistently maintained by believers in monism. If the former, the One would have contradictory natures — it is both essentially one and at the same time the foundation for plurality.

In short, a metaphysic which affirms that everything is either an appearance or a manifestation of the One is plagued with significant difficulties. Contrary to this view, it would seem that God is a distinct being, existing apart from the world. The world is his creation, created not out of himself but separate from himself. He enters it and relates to it, but it is not divine or part of the divine. There is an essential dualism — God and the world — and an essential pluralism — the separate existences of a plurality of beings. To reject pluralism for monism is, I think, to go against the primary testimony of our common experience.

25

Fourthly and finally, there is an objection similar to one posed against the second definition of immortality given above. Tillich's existential concern with the meaning of death and eternal life serves as a corrective to purely speculative accounts, but on the other hand leaves unanswered the historical question, "What happens after my historical death?" It is true that his query creates concern for how I live now, how I react to and involve myself in the meaning of what it is to be human in the present. But this concern must be balanced with an analysis of the *historical* future condition of the individual human person. Hence we turn to a fourth sense of "immortality."

Immortality as Individual Life After Death

I wish to suggest a fourth definition of immortality as an alternative to those above, namely, personal immortality. By "personal immortality" I mean "the actual survival of the individual human person, for an indefinite period after death, with that which makes for his own uniqueness (personal identity) and the awareness of such essentially intact."[13] This definition embodies four points.

First of all, the definition indicates that the individual *himself* will live subsequent to his death. On the one hand, he will possess the totality of elements or qualities which are essential to make him the same person that he was prior to his death. In his present existence there are certain features which are necessary to his being the particular person he is; these features constitute his criteria for personal identity. What these features are is a matter of dispute, but our definition does not commit itself to any particular answer to the difficult question about the nature of the criteria. It merely asserts that the individual will have those precise qualities which are essential to his personal identity in the life subsequent to his death, whatever they may be. On the other hand, he must have sufficient features to make him distinct from other people; he will not be part of the whole or God. He will still be human. Man has never been divine; he has only been created to be *like* the divine in certain respects. Thus, immortality means the survival of the individual as a discrete person, indeed, the same person as the one who died.

Secondly, the individual must have sufficient reason to think that he is the same person that he was prior to his death. That is, he must be *aware* of his self-identity. This can be ensured, at least in part, by his memory of his previous life. He must be able to remember a significant number of events of his life and recall many of the acts which he performed in that life. Likewise, he must be aware of significant personality and physical identities to his past constitution.

Thirdly, the extent of the duration of the life after death is left open. What is significant about our definition in light of the previous candidates is that we have returned true temporality to the notion of immortality. Immortality does take place in time; the individual will continue to exist subsequent to his death for a period of time.

Fourthly, the definition suggests that the individual *survives* death. The notion of survival as applied to death seems quite odd. "Survive" means "to remain alive or in existence." As a transitive verb it means "to continue to exist or function despite a particular condition or development." For example, "The dog survived the loss of his tail." When one applies this definition of "survive" to the above definition of "immortality," there is present an apparent contradiction. To say that a person survives his death means both that he *ceases* to exist or remain alive (he dies) and that he *continues* to exist or remain alive (he survives). In short, the very definition of immortality appears to make the event impossible because it contains a contradiction.

In view of this, it might be preferable to drop the term "survival," and replace it with "live subsequent to one's death." Whereas "survival" connotes continuous existence during and despite a particular condition or event, "life after death" has no such connotation. It simply means that dying is not the final event for the individual, that he will have experiences after his own death. If man is thought to possess a soul, the person may continue to exist despite death, or if man has no soul, he may come back to life. Which of these is actually the case must be left open until we discuss below the different views of the nature of man these notions presuppose. By introducing the term "live subsequent to one's death" we simply want to define "immortality" broadly enough to cover both cases, and yet avoid the apparent absurdities contained within the notion of "surviving one's death."

Accordingly, we can redefine "immortality" as "the actual existence of the individual human person for an indefinite period subsequent to his death, with that which makes for his own personal identity and the awareness of such essentially intact."

Immortality of this kind seems to me to be significant for several

27

reasons. First, not only can I *now* inquire whether such will actually be the case, but *in the future*, if it happens   I will be in a position to confirm or verify it (though obviously not to falsify it). Since immortality can in principle be verified, it is an empirical notion.

Likewise immortality thus defined can have moral significance for my present existence, for if the state or quality of my future existence depends, even in part, on my moral actions in my present life, this can be an incentive for certain kinds of moral activity. A promise of future rewards can encourage right action. Similarly, just as I now begin to prepare for my future, making plans and laying money aside so that I will have sufficient physical goods when I need them, there can also be moral and spiritual preparation for my future existence. In and of itself, of course, this definition of immortality does not have this implication. It must be linked with other assertions; for example, assertions about the existence of God, divine reward and punishment, and different states of future existence. However, the point is that this definition, combined with other such assertions, *can* have moral significance.

Accordingly, when we speak in this book about immortality, we are referring to it in this sense, that is, the sense of personal immortality, of personal life after death.

Exploring the Options

In the opening chapter we argued that the first question which must be dealt with is this: What must man be like for him to be capable of living subsequent to his death? The above discussion indicates that for there to be immortality the person who lives subsequent to his death must be the same person as the one who died. But what must man be like for the post-mortem person to be the same person he was before death? To answer this question we must explore at the outset of our inquiry the issue of the nature of man.

Traditionally, man has been viewed either as a unity or as a complex of physical and non-physical parts. The latter view comes down to us in the Western tradition from the philosopher Plato. Plato contended that man had two parts, a physical body and a non-physical (spiritual) soul. The body was responsible for the physiological activities of the human organism; to the soul were attributed the cognitive (thinking), conative (emotive), and appetitive activities of man. This position has been called dualism, because it contends that man is essentially composed of two different kinds of parts or entities.

Though Christian theologians and Western philosophers in the Platonic tradition have generally adopted a dichotomous view of man, some have suggested that man might be composed of more than two kinds of parts. For example, some have taken 1 Thessalonians 5:23 to suggest the trichotomous view that man is composed of three elements — body, soul, and spirit. Whether man is composed of two, three, or more kinds of parts I do not intend to explore. For our purposes, for any position which invokes, as a minimum condition, the presence of both a physical and a non-physical element in man, the issues which arise with respect to the problem of immortality are the same, no matter whether one views man as composed of only two or of more than two different kinds of elements. If immortality can be shown to be possible on the dualist view, the same considerations will apply to a trichotomous view of man. Similarly, the problems which arise for the dualistic view will occur in a trichotomous analysis. Accordingly, one of the options which we will consider with respect to the nature of man and his possibility for immortality will be the traditional position that man is to be dualistically conceived as possessing both a physical body and a non-physical element.

The other option, which we shall designate a monistic position, is likewise an ancient position, found in the writings of the Greek philosopher Aristotle. Though not without significant influence in the Christian tradition, particularly through the writings of Thomas Aquinas, this position has come into greater prominence and popularity in the twentieth century, first under the psychological theory called Behaviorism, and more recently, under the name Identity Theory. The latter claims that man is a physiological whole. It recognizes that there are two very different language systems used to characterize man, but affirms that these two language systems report one physical event, not two different events. We use a physical language to speak about man's brain, the electrical discharges and transfers of energy in it, and the central nervous system. Likewise, we use a psychological language about minds, ideas, concepts, and will. These two languages are mutually exclusive. For example, "that one has a tumor on his brain" means something quite different from the statement "he has a tumor on his mind." However, though the languages are distinct and non-interchangeable (there are brain surgeons, but not mind surgeons), it is a mistake to think that they refer to two different processes going on within the individual, conducted by two radically different entities. Rather, they are simply two language games which refer to one and the same physical event. Man is a psycho-physical unity.

Dualism and monism constitute the two views of the nature of man which we shall explore in the succeeding chapters, to see under what conditions man can or cannot live subsequent to his death. Dualism will occupy our attention in chapters three and four, monism in chapters five and six.

NOTES

1. *Reason in Religion* (N.Y.: Collier, 1962), pp. 174f.

2. It should be made clear that we are speaking here of death itself, not dying.

3. D.Z. Phillips, *Death and Immortality* (N.Y.: St. Martin's Press, 1970), p. 44.

4. *Ibid.*, p. 48.

5. *Ibid.*, pp. 54-55.

6. Chuang Tzu, *Chuang Tzu*, chapter 2 in Chan, ed., *A Source Book of Chinese Philosophy* (Princeton, N.J.: Princeton University Press, 1963), p. 190.

7. As with all sacred writings, there is a variety of interpretations of the *Upanishads*. I am presenting the *saprapanca* or cosmic view; the *nishprapanca* or acosmic interpretation is closer to the view of Tillich developed below, in which immortality has the existential meaning of discovering the reality of the present state of affairs, namely, the meaning of the unity of everything.

8. Paul Tillich, *Systematic Theology*, III (Chicago: University of Chicago Press, 1963), 398-401, 406-407, 410.

9. *Ibid.*, 399-400, 410; II, 67; I, 188.

10. *Ibid.*, 408-409.

11. *Ibid.*, 413-414.

12. *Ibid.*, 403.

13. Adapted from Corliss Lamont, *The Illusion of Immortality* (N.Y.: Philosophical Library, 1959), p. 22.

CHAPTER THREE

Dualism and Immortality

FREQUENT REFERENCES TO OUR OWN SELF AND TO THE SELVES
of others permeate our everyday speech. Consider, for example, the
following statements. I am making this maple rocking chair for myself. When I recovered from surgery, I was once more myself. I am
criticizing myself, not you. When he travels away from home, he
reveals his weaker self. She often tried to hide her true self by her
retiring mannerisms. When we use the term "self," about what are we
speaking? To what are we making reference?

At times, "self" is used in a purely reflexive sense to refer to our
entire being, as in "I painted that watercolor of Mt. Blanc myself."
However, the term "self" is also frequently used to indicate the real
me or the real person, as in "He never lets himself be known to
strangers." In this case my self is what I truly am.

Opinion varies on what the self, understood in this second sense,
is. To some, the self is the integrated unity of qualities, attributes,
characteristics, dispositions, and tendencies which are manifested in
the behavior of the individual. Others argue that there must be some
difference between the self and the characteristics manifested in overt
behavior, because the self can be distinguished from the manifest
behavior of the individual, as in the last example above. It, in some
sense or other, lies behind the behavioral characteristics or
manifestations.

Moreover, they go on to argue, the self must have some basis,
and that basis must be something other than the physical body visible
to other individuals. A scarred countenance may mask a peaceable
and gentle person, an ugly face or misshapen body a beautiful person.
Each of us wishes to protest the total identification of himself with his
physical appearance. In addition to the elements apparent to the

31

senses or visible to the surgeon there is a non-physical element which forms an essential part of man. The term "self" refers either to a part, function, or aspect of a substance or thing which is different in kind from the body, or to this substance in its entirety, either in itself or in its conjunction with the body. Thus conceived, man consists of two different kinds of elements: a physical body and a non-physical element variously called mind, ego, or soul.

The picture of man drawn here is the dualist one: man is a composition of both physical and non-physical elements. In this chapter I intend to develop this dualistic account of the structure of man, and then study its relation to the question of whether personal immortality is possible. To explore this dualistic view, we shall have recourse to the word "soul" and consequently to traditional concepts descriptive of the human soul. This might seem strange to some who are used to and prefer the term "self," particularly since one rarely finds the word "soul" used today outside of religious and theological discourse. However, since this thesis of the existence of a non-physical entity as an essential part of man is central to the view of man we wish to explore in this chapter, and since "soul" generally connotes a non-physical entity, whereas "self" does not, I propose to use "soul" rather than "self" to assist us in capturing the essence of the dualistic account. This term alone preserves the richness which this view of man embodies.

What Is the Soul?

"To attain any assured knowledge of the soul," Aristotle tells us, "is one of the most difficult things in the world."[1] One reason for this is that those who use the term "soul" rarely define it; the reader is left to glean its meaning from its usage in a multitude of contexts. One dualist who did render a definition was the Christian theologian Augustine, who defined the soul as "a special substance, endowed with reason, adapted to rule the body."[2] By noting that it is a special substance, Augustine seeks to set it apart as radically different from all physical objects. Whereas physical objects are characterized by having extensive properties (length, breadth, shape, texture) and being spatially locatable, the soul is non-physical, lacking physical properties or spatial coordinates. As an incorporeal entity, one cannot expect to encounter it in the world in the way one would a tree or a table.

However, Augustine argues, to say that the soul is non-physical or incorporeal is not to say that it is not a substance or a thing which really exists. Augustine likens it to justice.[3] Justice does not possess physical properties; it is not long or short, broad or deep. It cannot be encountered in the sensory world. Yet, he suggests, one would be loathe to deny that justice exists. So too, though the soul lacks physical properties, that does not entail that it is nothing and does not exist; a substance can be non-physical and still exist.

Unfortunately, this appeal to analogy will not support the weight placed on it. Augustine apparently thought that the word "justice" functions like other nouns in denoting or naming something. Since in the case of "justice" there is no physical object for it to name, it must name or denote something non-physical. But surely "justice," like the nouns "time," "goodness," and "truth," does not denote an existent, physical or non-physical. Indeed, all the inadequacies which Wittgenstein showed to plague a denotative system of language apply here.[4] On the other hand, though Augustine's use of the analogy of justice to support or illustrate his contention that "soul" names or denotes a non-physical object fails, the conclusion is, I believe, still true. There is no contradiction entailed in saying that something can be non-physical and still exist.

Nevertheless, to say that the soul is non-physical, immaterial, or incorporeal does not advance our understanding very far. It is merely to describe the soul negatively (via negativa), that is, by stating what it is not. Can anything positive be asserted about it?

Principle of Life

One way of understanding the notion of soul is in terms of its functions. In the beginnings of the Western philosophical tradition, one of the primary functions of the soul was to provide an explanation for life. As do we today, the ancients found the difference between living and non-living things intriguing and puzzling. The signs of life were seen to be various, according to the nature of the physical organism involved. For plants the signs were growth, nutrition, and decay; for animals, in addition to these, the powers of locomotion and sensation; for men all these plus knowing.[5] Since everything required a cause, the phenomena of being alive, of being able to feed oneself and grow, move about and sense the world, needed a cause. Matter alone, it seemed, could not be the source of these self-originating powers; as the potentiality for becoming something, matter needed to be actualized by a separate moving principle if it was to be living matter. This animating principle was the *animus* or soul.[6] The soul, therefore, was defined as the principle of life, and derivatively became the principle of self-originating motion.[7] It was that in virtue of which something was alive and could manifest the signs of life.

Though at one time this was deemed to be a most significant function, contemporary dualists rarely treat of it. This is due partly to the assignment of the life-giving powers to the physiological organism itself, and partly to the restriction of the application of "soul" to man alone.[8] Generally speaking, plants and animals are not viewed as having souls, though they are alive. Emphasis now is placed on the soul's ability to account for functions which purportedly cannot be fully explained by appeal to the human physiological structure. Accordingly, let us pass on to consider these other functions to see whether they can provide us with a positive description of the soul.

The Mind

More significant to the modern mind is a second function specified in Augustine's definition of the soul; it is, he writes, "endowed with reason." That is, it is responsible for the rational functions and intellectual capabilities of man.

In certain respects, human psychological processes are like those of animals. First, the senses of sight, hearing, feeling, taste, and smell are not unique to humans. Indeed, in other organisms one can find the employment of these senses much more highly refined. The eagle has superior sight, the dog smell, the deer hearing. The information gathered through these senses forms the basis of both men's and animals' perceptual experience of their environment. Secondly, animals, like man, can perform specific psychological operations upon the information which that perceived world presents to them. They are able to sort out the multitudinous sensory data received, discriminate and distinguish between what is presented, recognize that which has entered their perceptual field, and remember it. In doing this, they are capable of making perceptual abstractions and generalizations.[9] For example, when the rebus monkey is rewarded for pushing a triangularly shaped button, but punished for pushing a round one, he soon learns to discriminate which is which when the two are presented to him such that in his learning box he will, when presented with the two buttons, regularly push the triangularly shaped one. Likewise, he can generalize from this to new situations; even outside of his learning box he will consistently avoid round objects in favor of those shaped like a triangle.

But though animals are able to discriminate between various things presented in their sensory experience, such that they can recognize that two objects are similar or different enough to be reacted to appropriately, there is no reason to believe that they can understand the nature of the objects experienced. It would seem that they cannot recognize the *kind* of thing the perceived object is, and why it is the kind of thing it is. Neither do we have evidence that they can go beyond perceptual abstraction to classify the objects encountered, and discourse about those classifications — what they are and what they entail.

Man, on the contrary, possesses the capability not only of recognizing a perceived object as being of a certain kind, but also of knowing what that *kind* of thing is like. For example, man has both the perceptual ability to distinguish between different dogs, say a terrier and a spaniel, and the conceptual ability to know that a particular dog is a terrier and what it is to be a terrier as over against a spaniel. Possessing the power of concept formation, he can classify objects according to the kinds of things that they are, and can state what the necessary and sufficient conditions are for something to belong to that class.[10]

It would appear that this ability to form concepts is quite different from the ability to form percepts. First of all, percepts are formed only in the presence of the perceived object, and relate only to that which is perceived. I have a percept of the maple tree in my front yard only when I see it. Concepts, on the other hand, can be formed even when no perceptual object of this class is present. For example, I can form at this moment a concept of moon, and think about implied properties of moons, such as their globular shape and elliptical movements, though this is the middle of the day and no moon is visible to me. Moreover, I can form concepts of things which are intrinsically imperceptible. For example, I can form a concept of justice, even though there is no corresponding object which could be the object of any of my senses. This indicates that the processes used in concept formation must be different in kind from those involved in percept formation.

Secondly, a percept is always of a *particular* thing. We see a particular person; we hear a particular bird call on the lake; we taste the particular piece of chocolate we are now eating. But a concept is not of a particular thing; it is a general or abstract idea covering the essential characteristics of a class of things according to which particular things may be grouped. It is *universal* in that it extends over or includes the totality of things — past, present, or future, actual or possible — which might be subsumed under that class. For example, the concept robin is universal in that it includes all the robins that ever have, ever will, and could possibly exist. The word "robin" does not refer to one particular bird presently hunting worms in my back yard, but to a class of birds with orange breast feathers. Since concepts deal with classes, not particulars, the manner in which they are formed must be different from the manner in which percepts are formed. Again we have reason to assert that the ability to form concepts must differ in kind from the ability to form percepts.

As Descartes himself argued, evidence that man uniquely possesses this ability to form concepts is found in his possession of propositional language. Animals, it seems, are incapable of developing, utilizing, and understanding propositional language. They use *signals* which convey warnings or desires; they respond to signals which are cues for certain modes of behavior. But they do not use *symbols* as parts of speech which can be combined syntactically to form declarative sentences. Their language, verbal or non-verbal, does not possess anything similar to nouns, verbs, or adjectives which can be combined in different ways, such that an infinite number of discrete (distinctly meaningful) sentences can be constructed. Rather, their utterances are holophrastic; each utterance taken as a whole expresses something. The utterance cannot be varied in terms of any of its elements and still be meaningful;[11] a moose call blown with a trill in the middle is meaningless. Hence, animals cannot understand novel utterances and novel combinations. Human language, on the other hand, is a syntactical language. Man can construct, from his finite vocabulary and finite set of language rules, an infinite number of discrete sentences. Even sentences with the same elements in them can be distinguished in meaning by a variation of their syntactical relations. For example, note the identical words though different meanings of the following: She had a stolen book; She had stolen a book; She had a book stolen. Because of our ability to work with syntax, we can understand novel utterances and novel combinations of words. Most of the sentences in this book you have never before heard or read, yet you are capable of comprehending their meaning. This syntactical ability forms the basis for man's propositional language.

Since animal language consists only of signals, one need invoke nothing beyond perceptual abilities to account for their language behavior.[12] Signals must refer to something perceivable, and only operate meaningfully in the presence of particular perceptual situations. The frantic quacks of the mother duck to her fledglings upon the approach of humans are signs of a particular, perceived danger. To explain how the duck can formulate and understand these we need appeal only to the psychological level of perceptual abstraction and generalization.

But since human language is propositional, and contains symbols which denote classes of objects and which can inform about that which is either not now perceivable (as the moon) or in principle imperceptible (as goodness), we must appeal to a higher order of psychological explanation. It is man's psychological ability to form concepts that provides for the possibility of creating and using propositional language.[13]

Before we apply this to the question of the nature of the soul, we should take note of recent psychological experiments which tend to suggest that animals can use propositional language. Though attempts during the 1950's to teach chimpanzees to speak failed, current endeavors utilizing a different tack have proven more promising. Researchers have concentrated on teaching the apes to use a complex set of hand signals, pieces of plastic of different shapes and colors, or geometric designs on typewriter keys, rather than the spoken word, to communicate with their instructors.

For example, Beatrice and Allen Gardner and their former graduate student, Roger Fouts, have taught chimpanzees the American Sign Language, which was originally developed for use by deaf people.[14] It consists of hand gestures corresponding to individual words. By means of this language system they have taught one chimp, Washoe, a vocabulary of 160 words. Washoe can use this extensive vocabulary to sign a great variety of things, including things which are not physically present and (it is claimed) concepts. Most importantly, the chimps can combine these signs syntactically to communicate different ideas. For example, one chimp named Sarah is capable

37

of distinguishing between the combinations "red on green" and "green on red." This appears to indicate ability to understand elementary syntax, for the difference in meaning between the phrases depends not on the words alone, but also on their order. Further, they appear to be able to create novel, situation-appropriate combinations of signs to name new objects — Washoe called ducks "water birds," a combination of signs she invented — or to create their own sentences — Sarah stole symbols from her teacher to form her own questions, and then answered them.

In large part, however, the signs appear to be used by the chimps as signals and not as symbols. That is, with them the chimps signal their wants and desires, such as "gimme tickle," "open key" (locked door), or "go drink," or else respond to immediate, perceptual situations, usually created by the instructor. It would appear that one could explain their linguistic accomplishments by means of perceptual processes, without needing to appeal to the conceptual level. Of course, this research is in its elementary stages, and so preliminary judgments must be advanced cautiously and tentatively. Further work in this intriguing area must be awaited.

Returning to the question of the nature of the soul, if man alone can form concepts and discourse on the conceptual level, and if the ability to form concepts differs in kind from the ability to form percepts, there must be something unique about him which provides him with this additional ability. This ability is the power of conceptual thought — the ability to work with concepts or abstract ideas. Concepts are universals, that is, they extend over or include the totality of things which might be subsumed under that class. But nothing that exists physically is universal; all things which are in the physical mode of existence are particulars. The chair I am sitting on, the desk at which I am writing, the pen and paper I am using, are all individual particulars. Therefore, no concepts exist in the physical mode of existence. Concepts are non-physical or immaterial. As immaterial, they cannot be the object of or embodied in a physical organ, like the brain, for the physical works only with the physical. Neither can they be states of our nervous system, electrical discharges between brain synapses, or brain patterns. Consequently, that which works with or knows concepts must itself be a non-physical or immaterial thing.[15] And this immaterial thing is called the mind. Thus it is postulated that there exists in man a non-physical entity called the mind or soul,[16] one of whose functions is to provide man the capability of conceptually understanding and reasoning about his world.

This argument might be put in a slightly different fashion, but still make the same point. We have knowledge of things which are not physical and material, but immaterial. That is, we know things which are frequently abstracted from the here and now of existence. Such things are universals or classes, categories such as being, substance, and quality, non-sensible relations — for example, logical relationships of disjunction (or) or conjunction (and), genus and species — and the acts of knowing themselves, including inference and discursive reasoning. The fact that these objects of knowledge are not tied to any particular situation, to any here and now, means that they cannot be objects of sense knowledge or of physical activities, for these have to do with particular things in particular situations. Physical organs operate only with that which has particular existence. Therefore, we have knowledge which we cannot have in virtue of some physical organ. Thus, man knows by an act of knowledge which is not organic. The acts of knowing need a proper subject, that is, a knower. This subject cannot be a physical organism, in whole or in part, for the characteristics of physical organisms are to be extended and particular. Therefore, there must exist an immaterial subject, the intellectual soul, which has these abstract items as its objects of knowledge.[17]

The contention of these arguments, then, is that the soul is required to properly account for and explain the human power of conceptual thought. Man, like the animals, perceives his world, and this he does by use of physical organs. These organs work with data received as particular from that which exists in the particular, physical mode of existence. But man uniquely can go beyond the here and now to consider that which has a universal and immaterial mode of existence, that is, to form concepts, intentions, and non-logical relations which abstract from all particularity (in terms of the here and now). In order to know these, man must possess something more than his physical organs; he must have an immaterial mind or soul.

Recently a different argument has been suggested by Peter Geach in support of the non-physical basis of the mind. Geach argues that thinking is a discontinuous basic activity. "Each thought has a content that cannot pass over by a gradual transition to another content; if I have first the thought that lions are dangerous and then pass over to the thought that tigers are dangerous, this does not happen by a continuous change from the thought of a lion to the thought of a tiger. . . . Thinking consists in having a series of thoughts which can be counted off discretely — the first, the second, the third."[18] Therefore, "a thought cannot be significantly called long or short"; it is not extended over time. One cannot say that the thought lasted five minutes or thirty-five minutes. But physical processes, such as the basic activities of bodily organs or parts, can be measured in physical time. For example, one can say that it took me five minutes to digest the apple. Therefore, thinking is not a basic activity of a part of the physical body or of a bodily organ such as the brain. But, he goes on to argue, though thinking is not an activity of a material part of man, that does not mean that it is an activity of an immaterial part of man. "Thinking is a vital activity of a man, not of any part of him, material or immaterial."[19] Thus, though he argues for the immateriality of mental processes, he does not conclude from this to the existence of an immaterial entity like the soul.

However, this latter conclusion which Geach wishes to draw from his argument seems faulty. If the basic processes of bodily organs are measurable in physical time, it would seem that the processes of physical organisms, which are composed of physical parts and organs, would likewise be measurable in physical time. This is not because they are composed of organs whose processes are measurable, but because they are physical, just as the bodily organs are physical. It is because organs and organisms have a *physical* composition that their basic activities are measurable in physical time. Thus, if thinking cannot be a basic activity of a physical organ like the brain, it would seem that it cannot be a basic activity of a physical organism either. But if it is also not the activity of an immaterial part of man or soul (which Geach wishes to deny), then it is not the activity of anything, which is absurd. To have thinking without a thinker and reasoning without a reasoner is the same as having running without a runner and eating without an eater. Thus, either Geach's argument is fallacious, or else it confirms the dualist's contention that thinking is a basic activity of an immaterial part of man.

In summary, what we have argued in this section is that thinking and reasoning involve the unique human ability of concept formation. But this ability does not appear to be an ability characteristic of purely physical beings or capable of being performed by physiological organs. Thus, to account for man's unique ability to conceptualize, we must invoke the presence of an immaterial element called mind or soul. Accordingly, one of the most important functions of the soul is to provide for the human function of thinking and reasoning.

Moral Consciousness

A third function of the soul is related to the previous one. We have noted that concepts extend to the non-sensible, that man can form concepts which have no counterpart in the physical world. In particular, man's reasoning ability includes the capacity to form *moral* concepts. Man possesses a moral consciousness, such that in certain encounters in his world he realizes obligations and duties to perform the good or right action and avoid the wrong. In formulating decisions, he is aware not merely of the facts of the case under consideration, but likewise of the moral values which are involved. Ethical concepts such as good, bad, right, wrong, duty, and virtue, and ethical values such as justice, honesty, love, and self-sacrifice, constitute part of the stock of ideas which he brings to solve moral dilemmas. He not only knows these concepts and values, but is able to properly place these in moral judgments, avowing that certain actions are to be approved or disapproved. In making such judgments, his moral consciousness or conscience is involved; indeed, one might say that it is the conscience which makes such moral decisions, based upon the known facts of the situation and the values which form part of the individual's ideational structure. This capacity to form ideas of abstract values, to construct judgments about right and wrong from them, and to translate such into actual decisions resulting in moral behavior must be likewise attributable to the soul, as evidenced by the arguments in the previous section. As such, the soul functions in moral as well as non-moral intellectual understanding.

Furthermore, that which is involved in ethical decision-making *must* be something non-physical like the soul, for an adequate view of morality requires that the choice of the decision-maker be free. The complete reasoning behind this contention will be given in chapter six. Suffice it here to note that unless the moral choice be made freely, the individual who makes that choice cannot be held morally accountable for his choice and resulting action. If he could not have chosen otherwise than he did in fact choose, one cannot justly condemn him for not choosing to perform the other action, no matter how despicable the performed act was. But what is it to be free, to be able to have done otherwise? Human freedom entails that the individual not be completely determined by his biological composition or environmental factors. There must be a further, uncaused (by the biological or environmental) factor involved. This is the self. Freedom is self-determination. But if the self is to be free, it cannot be a physical entity, for that which is physical finds itself within the deterministic chain of causal conditions, biological and environmental. Hence, to be truly free, the self or soul must be non-physical. Thus, moral consciousness and moral decision-making require that man be more than merely a physical being; they require the presence of an entity such as the soul if man is to be able to make free moral choices.

Personal Identity

Fourthly, the soul is held to be the locus of the real person. Each of us is a particular and distinct individual persisting through time. We indicate this individuality or personal identity in a social context by assigning to each human being a different proper name or in this computer age a unique social security or account number. But what is it that makes us the unique person that we are and provides for the continuity of our person through time? What is the source of our personal identity?

The dualist suggests that our use of the first person pronoun in ordinary language provides a clue in this regard. The word "I" is used in at least two different ways. On the one hand, it is used to refer to the psycho-physical agent who is the speaker or writer of the sentence. For example, "I had a hard time trying to answer her questions"; "I went grocery shopping yesterday afternoon"; "He reads much more fluently than I do." On the other hand, "I" can be used more strictly to refer to the real person or self. For example, "My facial expression masks the way I truly feel"; "I have an old, crippled body." Here the "I" is distinguished from my observable facial or bodily characteristics. It refers to the true self, which is distinct from the physical. "I" as used in this second sense is the "I" of personal identity.

What is embodied here in our language, the dualist suggests, is the fact that personal identity is not to be found in my physical body. My posture, movement, and appearance express myself, but they are not the real person. They are the mode by which that person is manifested to others. By watching the bodily movements or gestures of another and by listening to what he has to say, I can make inferences to the nature of his real self. These are acts of revelation by which the true self is made known, but are not constitutive of the true self. The real person, the true self, must be non-physical; it must be located in or identical with the non-physical soul.

In reply to this argument it has been suggested that the "I" as used in the latter cases does not have a referential sense at all. It is like the word "there" in "There is a difference between jam and jelly." "There" does not refer to any spatial location, as it does in "You can park there." Similarly, though "I" has a referential sense when it is used in sentences which speak about the psycho-physical writer or speaker (as in "I went to the grocery store"), it has no referential sense in those cases where it seems to refer to something other than the physical being (as in "My facial expression masks the way I truly feel"). But on what grounds is it decided that the "I" has a referential sense in the former cases but not in the latter? Is it not simply the case that the critic has determined beforehand that terms function referentially only when that to which they refer can be known by sense experience, whereas they do not function referentially when the "referent" would be non-physical? Putting the reason this bluntly reveals, I believe, the true arbitrariness of this a priori criterion.

A second reason for concluding that the soul is the locus of personal identity comes from the contention that that which is the source of personal identity must be *essentially* unchanging. If it changes *in essence*, then that which makes me the individual that I am likewise changes, such that I am no longer the person I was previously. But the body is constantly undergoing alteration. The atoms which compose my present body will eventually be replaced by other atoms. I can even experience the loss of certain features of my body, such as my limbs or bodily organs. The heart of another or an artificial one can be substituted for my own; I can be given one of my brother's kidneys to replace one of mine that is not functioning. I can be fitted with a set of artificial arms or legs, or have my appendix removed. Yet even if all this occur, individually or all together, I would still sign checks with the same name and point to a particular birth certificate as my own. It is true that these events might alter my personality, but they would not affect my personal identity. I would still be my*self*.

Thus, the body cannot be the locus of personal identity.[20] That which provides the unchanging continuity necessary for personal identity must be the non-physical soul.

This is not to deny the importance or significance of the body. Since the self or soul lies hidden to all but our own selves, it must be revealed to others. The body is important in that it serves to manifest and express our true selves. It communicates to others the true individual which would otherwise lie unperceived and unperceivable. However, the soul, not the body, provides for my selfhood. Thus, the soul also functions in accounting for personal identity.

It has been objected to this that

> since the concept of [spiritual] substance is not an empirical one, there is no publicly usable set of devices for determining the continued presence of a [spiritual] substance, so its presence cannot serve as a criterion for applying the expression "the same person" in ordinary life.[21]

Moreover, not only does the soul provide an unusable criterion, but it is also merely a postulated metaphysical entity which, since it cannot be characterized, is completely devoid of content. "Its irrelevance to normal occasions for identity-judgments is due to its being merely an alleged identity-guaranteeing condition of which no independent characterization is forthcoming."[22]

To respond to the latter criticism first, we have tried in this chapter to establish that the soul is not completely devoid of independent characterization. If, as the dualist claims, the soul is the agent which is responsible for the cognitive activities already noted (since activities require an agent), then it is in part determinable by its dispositions to perform these activities. And this, in turn, helps us to respond to the former objection, for these very activities provide the means for discovering the nature and unique content of the individual soul. Though admittedly the soul per se is a non-empirical entity, it does become a usable criterion for identity when it manifests itself through the body. The body, in our present embodied condition, reveals to others the unique character traits, memories, and conceptual structures which are part of us, such that through their presence we can determine the continuity and identity of the person. However, one should not confuse the function of the body in providing the means for the manifestation of personal identity and the possibility of testing it, with the criterion or essence of personal identity. Personal identity is provided for not by the body, but by the persistence of personal, spiritual substance.

The Soul and the Body

Finally, Augustine's definition suggests that one function of the soul is to rule over the body. The body is inferior to the soul; it is the seat of appetites which tend to distract from the rational and moral activities of the soul. The flesh is opposed to the spirit, turning it aside from the pursuit of the highest goods and ideals, and engaging it in matters which are essentially temporal and not of lasting value. When the soul has control over the body, the good life will be achieved by emphasizing the spiritual, moral, and intellectual activities of man.

Self-control is impossible if man is nothing more than physical, or if the soul is simply the attunement or harmony of the parts of the body, for there is nothing to regulate the drives and impulses of the body. One cannot expect the body to control the body. Therefore, the soul must be independent of and able to govern the body in order for man to manifest the power of self-mastery and self-control essential to becoming a moral individual.

That the soul can rule over the body in such a way that it can control its members, raises the question of the precise relation of the body to the soul. That is to say, is the body a necessary condition for the existence of a soul, or can the soul exist completely independent of the physical organism?

On the one hand, most dualists have affirmed that the soul is capable of an existence independent of the body.[23] There are certain processes which, since they are due to the conjunctive activity of body and soul, require the presence of a body. For example, sensory perception requires both the soul to recognize or be aware of the perceived data, and the appropriate physical organs to receive the stimulus. Physical eyes are necessary for vision, ears for hearing. However, other mental processes, such as thinking, which is the highest function of the soul, *can* occur without the accompanying performance of a physical organ (though in our present embodied state it does have the accompanying performance of the brain). In particular the mental functions of reasoning, understanding, and willing can be performed by a disembodied soul.

On the other hand, those who have held the above view at the

45

same time have acknowledged the significant mutual influence which the body and mind have on each other. The body does indeed affect the mind, for it supplies the basic data with which the mind works. We abstract from our experience of particular things encountered in our environment to form concepts. Without this relevant experience, we could never know about our world. Similarly, our will, though free, chooses between alternatives presented to it by our experience. From the information supplied to it by past experience or the communicated experience of others, it concludes that a certain course of action should be opted for.

A clear example of this kind of influence can be found in communication between individuals. Through your sensory organs you hear what I have to say. This sensory information is in turn conveyed to your mind, organized in terms of your past experience and understood. Thus, your physical environment has caused certain events to occur in your mental world. Likewise, my mental world, in communicating my ideas to you, has caused certain events in the physical realm, for organic movements and sounds have occurred as a result of my desire to communicate with you.

The conclusion to be drawn from this is that though the body is not a necessary condition for the *existence* of the soul, it is a necessary condition for many of the *functions* and processes in which the soul is involved. Though the soul can exist without the body, in such a state it is incomplete; its functions are so severely limited that to attain complete fulfillment it must ultimately be reunited with the body. Only in a bodily state can man achieve complete happiness.

To sum up, man consists of at least two elements: a physical organism which can be sensed and a non-physical entity which cannot be sensed, though its presence is manifested as the personhood of each of us. This non-physical entity functions as our mind and as the principle of personal identity (as that which makes us the persons that we are). Though at present the soul does exist embodied, most dualists hold that it can exist in a disembodied state as a distinct, conscious, living person, though in such a state man is incomplete.

Application to the Possibility of Immortality

Building upon the above analysis, we are provided with an excellent candidate for human immortality. Dying is a physical process. But the soul is not a physical entity. Hence, the existence of the soul cannot be affected by physical death; the soul cannot die. The corruption of the body, of course, would affect those functions which require the mutual involvement of both the physical and the non-physical, as in sensation. The destruction of the physical partner would mean that the soul would have within it the power of perceiving, but it would lack the physical organs to implement and complete this activity. However, the existence of the soul and those functions which are not dependent upon the physical, as intellect and will, would remain unaffected (except by lack of additional empirical input) by the destruction of the physical.

Secondly, though in the present life the soul is conjoined to the physical body in such a manner that the physical and mental can best function together, the latter ultimately is capable of existing independently of the physical. Hence, the destruction of the physical leaves the mental essentially intact. In particular, this applies to self-consciousness. Since the self is the soul and is non-physical, I can be aware of myself apart from the physical requirements of sensation. That is, I am immediately or intuitively aware of who I am. Thus, the destruction of the sense organs does not affect my awareness of who I as a person am. This is particularly important in light of the fact that awareness of oneself is an essential feature of a doctrine of personal immortality.

Similarly with memory. The memory is also capable of functioning apart from the sensory. It is true that the sensory is responsible for the initial data input, but after the input the memory is able to recall that bit of data apart from the use of the senses. Even with my eyes closed I can recall visually the form and appearance of my house; I can visualize its contents and their particular characteristics. Thus, the power of memory likewise remains in the soul to function subsequent to death. Again, this is crucial for the doctrine of immortality, for memory is necessary in order for there to be an awareness that the individual now existing is the same person that died; one must be able to remember his past life, experiences, and events in order to recognize that he is still the same individual.

Thirdly, we noted above that the soul provides the locus for personal identity. It is that which makes me the person that I am; it is the center for my personality and character. Hence, the dualistic doctrine provides for the *personal* existence of the individual after his

47

physical death. The person lives on, even though his body has died.

From this analysis it can readily be seen that this view of man provides a candidate for human immortality as we have defined it. With its doctrine of the non-physical soul as the person, dualism provides for the possibility of the continued existence of the real person for an indefinite period after death. Since the soul is the real person and cannot die a physical death, the existence of the real person remains unaffected by bodily death and corruption. Dualism also provides the ingredients enabling an individual to know that he is the same person as the one whose body died. He would know it, first, because there is temporal continuity between the individual prior to and after his death. He will be continually and intuitively aware of himself because that which lives on is the conscious soul. Secondly, since the soul as mind is the locus of memory, he will be able to recall his past. Having fulfilled our criteria, if dualism is correct, if man has a soul, and if that soul is the person — if man *is his soul* — personal immortality is possible.

Three points should be noted in conclusion. First, this view of man allows us to reintroduce the notion of survival into the question of life after death. It will be recalled that in chapter two it was objected that the term "survival" was inappropriately used in this regard, for "survive" means to continue on in existence, whereas the person in death did not so continue. Thus, it was argued, language about survival leads to an inherent contradiction. However, if one takes a dualistic viewpoint, language about survival, if carefully employed, can be reintroduced meaningfully. It is not I who die, but my body. Hence, the real I does continue to exist despite the decease and corruption of the body. Death does have a survivor in the person of the soul. Accordingly, to say that someone survived his death is a (bad) way of stating that though his body die, he in the person of his soul continues to exist subsequent to that bodily event.

Secondly, that man can be immortal, that his soul is not affected by physical death, does *not* mean that he can be *assured* of eternal life or even of life after death. This might seem an odd conclusion, following upon the assertion that the soul does not die. However, though the existence of the soul cannot be affected by physical deterioration, it does not follow that it might not be capable of being affected in ways other than by physical disintegration. If one accepts the assertion that the soul at some time came into existence, there might be some analogous way in which it could be annihilated. The possibility of immortality should not be confused with the actuality of it. The doctrine of the soul shows that man is constituted such that by possession of a soul he *can* be immortal; that is, that he does not die when his physical body dies. Whether he actually is immortal, whether the soul does continue to exist subsequent to physical death, we will have to explore in a later chapter.

Finally, the manner in which the soul exists after death remains somewhat problematic. Several options are possible. First, if the soul is self-sufficient, it can continue to exist in and of itself, needing no physical counterpart. Thus, the life after death would be a disembodied one, with disembodied souls knowing other disembodied souls. Though this has been maintained by some, the Christian view is that the soul is incomplete without the body. The body seems to be too important a part of our humanity to be so readily and forever disposable. If life after death is to an embodied life, a resurrection of some sort is essential. Accordingly, a second view is that the soul continues to exist after the death of the physical body, until such time as it is reunited with a resurrected or re-created body. Here again there is a diversity of opinion, both about the body with which it is reunited and the time of the reunification. Some have held that the body which is reunited with the soul is the self-same body which died.[24] I cannot be myself without my original body, and without a union with the self-same body there is no resurrection. Hence the atoms of this mortal body will be collected and re-united by God. However, those who hold this also generally claim that the body will be perfected by God in the afterlife; hence some changes in the body will be forthcoming. Others have held that since the body can be destroyed by cremation, or even have its atomic particles become part of another body (as in cannibalism), simple resurrection is impossible. Accordingly God will re-create or reconstruct a new body for the soul similar to the original body. For some this re-created body is physical; for others it is a spiritual body. As to the matter of time, though some have believed that the soul acquires a body immediately upon death, it is most generally maintained in the Christian tradition that the time of the resurrection or re-creation is future. The soul continues to exist independently for a time, until the eschatological resurrection or re-creation of the body occurs. As can be seen from this diversity of opinion, though immortality is possible on this view of man, the

49

nature and manner of it remain to be determined. We shall have more to say on this in the next and final chapters.

NOTES

1. *De Anima*, Bk. I, ch. 1 (402a10).

2. *The Greatness of the Soul* (London: Longmans, Green & Co., 1950), chapter 13, par. 22.

3. *Ibid.*, chapter 4, par. 5.

4. Ludwig Wittgenstein, *Philosophical Investigations* (N.Y.: Macmillan, 1953), Pt. I, par. 1-26, 40-45.

5. Aristotle, *op. cit.*, Bk. II, chapters 2 & 3.

6. In Latin, *"animare"* (from which we get "animate") means to quicken, enliven, or endow with a soul.

7. Plato, *Phaedrus*, 245e; *Cratylus* 397d-e, 400a.

8. One finds such a move in René Descartes: "All the actions of brutes resemble only those of ours that occur without the aid of the mind. Whence we are driven to conclude that we can recognize no principle of motion in them beyond the disposition of their organs and the continual discharge of the animal spirits that are produced by the beat of the heart as it rarefies the blood. At the same time we shall perceive that we have no cause for ascribing anything more to them . . . ." "Reply to Objections IV," *Philosophical Works of Descartes*, II (N.Y.: Dover Pub., 1934), 104.

9. Mortimer J. Adler, *The Difference of Man and the Difference It Makes* (N.Y.: World Pub., 1967), pp. 152-154.

10. *Ibid.*, chapter 11.

11. One possible exception to this is the dance of the honey bee. By means of the speed and angle of the dance they communicate the distance and direction of the source of the nectar. However, the variations in the dance are not in kind, but in degree, such that it would hardly qualify as a propositional or syntactical language. See *ibid.*, pp. 114-118.

12. *Ibid.*, pp. 152-164.

13. *Ibid.*, chapter 11.

14. Joyce Fleming, "The State of the Apes," *Psychology Today* (January, 1974), pp. 31-46.

15. Adapted from Adler, *op. cit.*, pp. 220-222, 340-347.

16. For Augustine, the soul is the vivifying principle of the body, whereas the spirit (mind) is the power of rational thought and understanding. However, these are not two distinct entities, but one. The spirit, taken in the

sense of mental functions, is a part of the soul; however, "spirit is synonymous with soul in its general sense." *On the Soul and Its Origin*, Bk. IV, ch. 37.

17. Adapted from Duns Scotus, *Philosophical Writings*, trans. Allan Wolter (Indianapolis: Bobbs-Merrill, 1964), pp. 148-154. This argument can also be found in Augustine (*The Greatness of the Soul*, ch. 13, par. 22) and in the Scholastics in much the same form.

18. Geach, *God and the Soul* (N.Y.: Schocken Books, 1969), pp. 34-35.

19. *Ibid.*, p. 38.

20. Locke distinguished between the identity of the man and personal identity. The former involves bodily continuity, whereas the latter necessitates consciousness of one's past (memory). That personal identity differs from the identity of the man can be seen in that "the *substance* whereof personal self consisted at one time may be varied at another, without the change of personal identity; there being no question about the same person, though the limbs which but now were a part of it, be cut off." *An Essay Concerning Human Understanding*, Book II, ch. 27, par. 11.

21. Terence Penelhum, *Survival and Disembodied Existence* (London: Routledge & Kegan Paul, 1970), p. 76.

22. *Ibid.*

23. The dualistic position which maintains that the body is a necessary condition for both the existence and functioning of the soul will be considered in the next chapter.

24. Thomas Aquinas, *Summa Theologica*, Supplement to the Third Part, Q. 79, A. 2.

CHAPTER FOUR

Critique of Dualism

In the previous chapter we described dualism, presented the arguments which are frequently given in its behalf, and concluded that on this view of the nature of man personal immortality is possible. However, is this view of man defensible? Is it reasonable to believe that man actually possesses or is a soul? The dualistic thesis is not without its difficulties. There is not space enough, neither is it within the purview of this book, to develop them all. However, in the following pages I intend to point out four difficulties, concentrating mainly on those which have a bearing on the question of immortality. Though they do not disprove the dualistic thesis, they do call into serious question its main tenets.

The Question of Death

The first problem which confronts the dualist is the difficulty of providing an adequate and reasonable account of human death, and of reconciling it with our ordinary language about a person's death. Those who maintain the existence of the soul entity in man contend that though the physical body die, the soul does not. The soul survives the decease and corruption of the physical organism or shell, thus providing the possibility of immortality. Moreover, as we noted in chapter three, it is the soul which is the real self. Unless the criterion for personal identity be found in the soul, that which is immortal is not I. Consequently, since the soul is the real person, and since the soul is not subject to death, no individual person ever dies.

How then are we to interpret the event of death? Death must consist of two aspects. From the point of view of the body, death is the cessation of the vital functions of the organism. The heart stops pumping blood, the lungs cease to move air, the nervous system no longer transmits impulses to and from the brain. The body begins to decompose. But since I am not my body, I as the real person do not undergo death. For the soul or real person, death is the release of the soul from the body. Only the dying of my body is experienced. In other words, not John Smith the person, but John Smith's body, dies.

Now at the outset this is indeed a strange notion, quite contrary to our ordinary manner of speaking. Take, for example, the statement: (A) "My uncle died at the age of 80." The subject of this proposition is the person who was my uncle, and what is described is his death — the death of him as a person. However, if we adhere to the doctrine of the existence of a soul in every man, the person, as a non-physical soul, cannot die. In order then to express the event of my uncle's decease, the above statement is inappropriate. Whereas it indicates that the person of my uncle died and is now dead, if he exists as a souled being, though his body be dead, he himself continues to exist, presumably in some spiritual realm. Consequently, we must rephrase A as follows: (B) "My uncle's heart, lungs, and brain ceased functioning at the age of 80, but he (as a person) lives on."

But note how different this second statement is from the first. On the one hand, statement B leaves the reader confused in that its two constituent propositions appear to be self-contradictory. Whereas one of its propositions claims that my uncle lives on, the other describes the termination of the functioning of his heart, lungs, and brain, which are usually accepted as the criteria for a person's death. Thus, the proposition appears to assert that though the criteria for his death are present, my uncle is not dead. This is not to say that for the speaker of the statement it is self-contradictory, for the criteria could be interpreted as the criteria, not for the death of the person, but solely for the death of the body. However, to use these criteria as referring *only* to the bodily aspect of the deceased is contrary to our ordinary use of these important criteria in death statements, as, for example, "John Smith died of a brain hemorrhage."

On the other hand, statement B is quite a different statement from A, for whereas the second part of proposition B affirms that my uncle is still alive, proposition A affirms that he really is deceased. If we adopt the view that man is a souled being, we must radically alter our ordinary manner of speaking about human death, such that only language which describes the death of the physical organism — as

53

over against the continued life of the person — is acceptable. The number of changes required in our linguistic utterances would be great; indeed, there would probably remain few death statements untouched by this alteration. The overhauling of our language would extend from newspaper obituaries to physicians' prognostications. But before we attempt such radical surgery on our language, we should question the view of man itself which forces us to make such drastic changes.

Secondly, the doctrine that man as a person does not die poses particular difficulties for the *Christian* dualist. For one thing, it is apparently contrary to the teachings of Scripture. "It is appointed unto men once to die." "If we live, we live to the Lord, and if we die, we die to the Lord." "For as in Adam all die, so in Christ shall all be made alive." Each of these and numerous other passages indicate that each of us, as a person, must die. There is no hint that the only thing spoken about is the destruction of the physical organism, and that the real person, the soul, does not die but lives on.

Indeed, when the New Testament writers speak of resurrection, it is always in terms of the resurrection of the *individual* from the dead. Never is it stated as resurrection of the body alone. It is not merely dead bodies that are raised; it is the dead persons themselves, with their bodies, that are given new life. We are mortal; resurrection from the dead will be *to* immortality.[1]

Furthermore, if the individual does not die, then Jesus Christ himself did not die. Yes, his body ceased to function, but the real person of Jesus, his soul, did not die. But if such be the case, what becomes of the bulwark of Christianity? "Christ died for our sins," must be given the lie. When Paul makes this affirmation in I Corinthians 15:3, he means more than that the bodily functions of Jesus ceased and that his body began to decompose. The subject of "died" acts as the subject of the verbs which follow: buried, raised, and appeared. If only his body died and not his person, then only his body appeared to the disciples and not his person, a position unacceptable to Christians. Paul's claim is that the individual, Jesus Christ, died. Interpreted dualistically, this leads to the impossibility that his soul died. But for the dualist the soul cannot die; it as non-physical provides the very possibility for continued existence. Thus the Christian believer in the soul is faced with a dilemma: either the soul is capable of dying, in which case it cannot be the candidate which provides for the immortality of man, or else, since the soul is undying, Christ did not die "and you are still in your sins."

A Reply

Some dualists have replied to this objection by revising what was said in the previous chapter regarding personal identity. There we noted the dualist position that the soul and the soul alone is responsible for personal identity. I am essentially my inner self or soul; the body merely serves to express or inform it. Some dualists take exception to the extreme Platonism of this view. An individual person, they argue, is essentially soul and body. The combination of body and soul makes me the person that I am. Death involves the separation of the soul and body, and consequently the death of myself. There is something which does not die, namely the soul, but this is only a truncated person, incomplete in itself. "When they separate, the body is not in any sense a person. . . . The soul is still a person but a damaged, a mutilated person, lacking many things proper to a human person."[2] To restore wholeness, the re-creation of the body is essential.

Two objections might be raised against this revised view. First, is it legitimate to say that that which survives is a person at all, even if only a truncated person? If, as is the case in this revised view, the body is necessary for personal identity, there can be no person without both body and soul. John Smith, while he was alive, was a particular person because he possessed a particular body and a particular soul. But all that remains after death is a soul. If the body is necessary for being a human person, this soul cannot be the person, John Smith. Hence, that which survives death is either impersonal or apersonal. Furthermore, if there are to be relationships between souls or between souls and God in this intermediate state, they cannot be *personal* relationships. This consequence seems unacceptable, for an impersonal immortality has no more significance for me as a person than would the indefinite preservation by a medical school of my apersonal heart or appendix in formaldehyde.[3]

Secondly, personal immortality, as defined above, requires the existence of the individual human person subsequent to his death. But only a part of me lives on; I as a *person* do not survive. Therefore, dualism so understood provides no candidate for personal immortality.

The first objection, the dualist might reply, yields no important criticism of his position. The difficulty here envisioned is only a terminological one. If one chooses to call the composite of body and soul a person, then one cannot call the surviving soul a person or make it personal. But this is only a matter of naming it. That which survives is still conscious, able to think and know, and a part of me. Thus, this intermediate state does have significance for me, for it is my conscious part which lives on, the part that can be aware of itself and of others. Whether one chooses to call it personal or not does not matter.

However, the issue is not merely terminological. If the body is necessary for personal identity, that which lives on is not me, and further it is a mistake to say that the surviving soul continues to be a part of *me*, or is *my* soul. It is true that it was formerly part of me. But with the separation of my body and soul, I, John Smith, no longer exist. Hence, something cannot belong to or be a part of me. For example, I might say that this gold watch *was* my grandfather's; but since he as a person does not now exist, I cannot say it *is his* watch, for there is no "he" to have possessions. Consequently, it is not *my* soul that continues to exist, but simply *a* soul. Thus, tracing the history of the conscious soul would seem not to differ from tracing the history of one of my bodily organs or physical atoms after death. After I die it would continue on its own course, developing and changing in its own way. But this kind of continued existence has no significance for me. It is simply *an* atom, *a* heart, *a* soul.

To the second objection the dualist might reply that the continuance of a part of me — my consciousness — is sufficient to provide a candidate for future immortality, though it is not itself an immortal person. Personal immortality really begins at the resurrection. The intermediate state is incomplete at best. It merely functions to provide the continuity between bodily death and the resurrection or re-creation of the body required to establish personal identity.

But is it sufficient? I think not. To see this, let us for a moment suppose that that which continued to exist was not the conscious soul but rather the body. Suppose that at my death the University of Minnesota preserved my body for further study, and that at some future time God creates another soul and joins it to this body. Would this new creation still be me?

To answer this, let us suppose that the soul which is re-created and joined to the preserved body differs significantly from the soul which died. It would remember some things differently and some new things, would have significantly different characteristics, and would think with additional or changed patterns and concepts. Would not this re-created person be a different person from the individual who died? And would not the reason which we would give for this be that, though the physical elements were continuous, it has different concepts, ideas, personality, and memories? In short, mere continuity of body would not be sufficient to establish personal identity.

Returning to the case at hand, suppose that there is some continuous non-physical substance, say a soul, which at some future time is conjoined to a body. As we have argued above, this soul, though formerly a part of me, is no longer mine or related to me, since I no longer exist. It is merely *a* soul, which in the time since it was separated from my body at death has acquired new thoughts and ideas, new memories and characteristics.[4] As such, would not this re-created person be a different person from the individual who died? And would not the reason which we would give for this be that, though there was a continuous non-physical element, it has different concepts, ideas, personality, and memories? In short, mere continuity of non-physical, apersonal substance (soul) would not be sufficient to establish personal identity.

Our contention here is that this revised view of dualistic man resolves the problem of death, but at the price of introducing serious difficulties with respect to that which continues on in the state intermediate between death and resurrection or re-creation of the body. The soul that exists and develops during this period is not personal and has no significance for or continuing relation to me. Neither is it sufficient to establish personal identity at the resurrection or re-creation. The result has been to trade one solution for a handful of other problems.

This, of course, is not a fatal objection to this revised dualistic view as a theory of the nature of man. It simply means that if defenders of this view intend to maintain that man is immortal, they cannot account for or provide for it along the traditional dualist lines developed above (that is, in terms of the preservation of the person as a soul). Neither can they talk meaningfully of a person existing in some state intermediate between death and re-creation. The possibility of immortality will depend upon the possibility that the person can be re-created to be the same person as the deceased, a notion which we will explore in the next chapter.

Is the Body Necessary?

The second problem arises from a conflict between the dualistic view of the possibility of disembodied mental activity and contemporary scientific conclusions about the necessity of the body for consciousness. The dualist contends that man has a soul which can be immortal; though the body die, the soul continues to exist.

Moreover, we are assured that reunification with a body does not occur immediately upon death. In his "Myth of Er" Plato speaks of the long journey of the soul between earthly death and reincarnation.

> Er saw the souls which had been judged departing by one of the openings in the sky and one of those in the earth; while at the other two openings souls were coming up out of the earth travel-stained and dusty, or down from the sky clean and bright. . . . Greetings passed between acquaintances, and as either party questioned the other of what had befallen them, some wept as they sorrowfully recounted all that they had seen and suffered on their journey under the earth, which had lasted a thousand years; while others spoke of the joys of heaven and sights of inconceivable beauty.[5]

The Christian Scriptures recount that the resurrections of Jesus and Lazarus did not occur until three days after their deaths. Likewise, Paul in II Timothy 2:18 refutes the error that the resurrection from the dead has already occurred. Accordingly, since the resurrection of and reunification with the body is future, death must be followed by an indefinite period during which the soul continues to exist in some disembodied state. We might diagram this as follows:

Physical death	Persistence of the soul without a body	Reunification of the soul with the (re-created or resurrected) body

Furthermore, dualists seem to hold that during this time the soul continues to perform its essential functions of thinking and willing. Plato leaves no doubt about this, for these souls have the opportunity

to choose the life of their reincarnation during this time. The Scriptures are less clear on this, depending particularly upon whether one
interprets Luke 16 as depicting a real situation, or as merely a
parabolic story using imagery common to the people of that time. In
any case it is clear that most Christian dualists hold to a cognitively
active soul during this intermediate state.

During this time the soul's cognitive functions continue in much
the same manner as before, except that now it is limited by the lack of
perceptual powers to introduce new sensory input or by the lack of a
body to carry out its volitions. Dualists suggest, for example, that the
soul would be aware of itself, understand its present condition, and
remember its past so as to know that it is the same as the individual
who died. The Christian doctrine of immortality stresses a God-
relationship as much as, if not more than, mere temporal persistence,
such that it would be conscious of God as well.

Granted these three contentions — that the soul continues to
exist after physical death, that the resurrection or reunification does
not occur at the time of bodily death, and that the soul in that state
continues to exercise certain mental capacities — it seems to follow
that the dualist must assert that the body is not a necessary condition
for cognitive processes.

One, however, must be careful about the way in which this
assertion is understood. Most traditional dualists affirm that the soul
can exist in a disembodied state with full consciousness of itself and
with its conceptual and intellectual abilities, but at the same time
contend that such a person is not a complete individual until he be
reunited with the body. In other words, the body is a necessary condition for *completeness*, in the sense that there are many human functions which can not be performed unless the soul exist within a body.
These functions include perception and, for some thinkers, imagina-
tion. In these cases the body is a necessary condition for the appropriate mental activity. At the same time the body is not deemed a
necessary condition for those functions which are appropriate only to
the soul. Since the soul during its disembodied state will be able to
understand, know intuitively, and be self-aware, these cognitive activities apparently do not require the presence of the body. Thus, it
seems that the dualist is contending that the body is not a necessary
condition for such cognitive activities as self-consciousness, understanding, reasoning, and remembering.

The difficulty which arises is this: scientific evidence seems clearly to indicate that the body is a necessary condition for the existence and function of human consciousness. Evidence for such a conclusion comes from a variety of areas.

First, studies indicate that certain mental abilities and the degree to which they function successfully are in part inherited. For example, researchers have correlated the intelligence of members of natural families. Their data discloses that the highest correlation exists between identical twins; it progressively diminishes, though remains significant, for fraternal twins, siblings, parents and children, grandparents and grandchildren, and cousins. The farther removed the genetic relation, the lower is the intelligence correlation. This indicates that heredity plays a major role in determining mental ability. Since heredity is a physical process working through genes and chromosomes, the physical appears to be a necessary condition for the mental.

Secondly, damage to the brain has a direct effect upon consciousness, memory, and conceptual ability. A blow on the head can result in loss of consciousness. A more severe blow can destroy brain tissue. This concussion can lead to amnesia, and ultimately to the inability to form abstract concepts. Research done by the psychologist Kurt Goldstein on patients who suffered severe brain damage in World War I indicated that such damage greatly affected their ability to abstract. They were unable, for example, to detach their ego from their world of experience. When a patient was asked to repeat the statement, "The snow is black," he refused to do so, since snow is not that color. He was unable to remove himself from his concrete experience of snow to consider an abstract possibility or idea. Similarly, patients were unable to account for abstract spatial relationships. Though they were able to point to spatial directions which could be perceived, such as up and down, they were unable to verbalize the notion of abstract space. Goldstein's experiments show that there exists a direct connection between the brain and mental processes, such that damage to the brain can and does affect conceptual abilities.

Thirdly, feeble-mindedness, which is a condition of the intellect, can result from physical causes. Lack of oxygen before or at birth can severely damage the brain of the infant, and consequently affect its intelligence. Another cause of feeble-mindedness may be a single defective gene. There is a gene which is responsible for the production of an enzyme which is instrumental in disposing of an acid produced by the brain's activity. When this gene is defective, the chemical reaction by which the brain eliminates this acid is blocked, and the acid accumulates in the brain. The consequence of this accumulation is a kind of feeble-mindedness called *phenylpyruvic oligophrenia.* This shows that intellectual ability depends directly upon the condition of the physical environment and/or the physiological organ.

Further, there are areas of the brain in which sensory activities can be located. Stimulation of certain rear parts of the cerebral cortex has an effect on vision, enabling the patient, for example, to perceive certain colors not present to other observers. Areas governing hearing are located in the middle section of the cortex which is associated with the receiving of sound. This, of course, simply serves to show that *perceptual* abilities are associated with localized brain activities. What is the evidence with respect to *conceptual* abilities?

There appears to be no specific brain localization of these abilities. For example, there is no specific center in the brain associated with learning or memory. However, research has established the vital role of the physiological with respect to both of these abilities. With regard to the former, it indicates that a crucial factor in the learning process is protein synthesis in the brain. Rats undergoing training produced greater amounts of certain nervous-system proteins in the beginning of their learning experience, when they were attempting to cope with the learning problem. More directly to our question, protein deficiencies in children have marked negative effects upon their learning abilities. With memory, though it appears to be spread throughout the cortex, it is significantly affected by the part of the brain called the hippocampus. If this is destroyed or partially removed, the individual cannot recall new information.

Recent physiological studies of the brain also show that intelligence, though not specifically localized, is associated with specific cerebral hemispheres. Research suggests that there is not one but two different kinds of intelligence, each with its own general brain location. Analytic, conceptual, verbal intelligence is apparently located in the left hemisphere of the brain. This side would control many of the mental processes which we have been discussing above. But the right hemisphere is responsible for and controls the artistic and intuitive mental processes, including the ability to synthesize ideas. Usually one hemisphere is dominant over the other. Consequently, individuals will frequently manifest or excel in one kind of intelligence function as over against the other.

Finally, the action of physical diseases upon the brain, intellect, and personality points to this conclusion. For example, syphilis is a disease produced by an infection by a microorganism. This microbe enters the body and forms lesions, which in turn eventually can cause personality changes, such as forgetfulness, apathy, or violent rages, even convulsions. Likewise, if it attacks and destroys the brain, it causes mental changes, loss of memory, lack of insight, and eventually insanity. Another example of the dependency of the mental on the condition of the physical is cretinism, which results from the failure of the thyroid gland to secrete enough of its hormone. Deficiency of this hormone produces not only the physical consequences of arrested growth and organic development, but also serious mental deficiency. Even though the physiological condition is recognized and treated later, mental deficiency and even imbecility will persist. The effects of these diseases upon the mental abilities of the individual provide clear indication that the mental is dependent on and to some extent determined by the physical condition of the body.

Much other evidence could be marshalled, but we have seen sufficient information to show that overwhelming psychological and physiological evidence points to the fact that the brain and central nervous system are necessary conditions for the functioning of mental processes such as abstraction, reasoning ability, concept formation, and memory. Indeed, there is no evidence at all to suggest that the mental can exist and function independently of the physiological.

If this be the case, then a dilemma confronts those who maintain the presence of the soul in man. Either they must deny that the soul continues to be conscious and perform cognitive activities after death, or else they must deny the mass of psychological and physiological evidence which indicates that the body is necessary for the existence of the mind and the performance of cognitive activities. The latter option seems unacceptable in light of contemporary scientific knowledge. The former likewise seems impossible if one is to hold to the existence of a soul, for the removal of its ability to perform conscious activities would effectively disembowel it of its nature and functions. It would no longer serve as the foundation for thought, moral consciousness, or personal identity; all that would remain would be its animating capacity. Moreover, it could no longer provide for the possibility of personal immortality, for it would lack the necessary features of self-consciousness, memory, and awareness of personal identity.

One might seek to avoid this dilemma by maintaining that during this intermediate state the soul is given a body with which to function. This ethereal body comes to the soul immediately upon the death of the physical body. However, first of all, there is no evidence that there exists any such body; surely if it existed there would be some evidence pertaining to it. Secondly, such a claim would seem to make future bodily resurrection unnecessary. One already would possess a body; thus one would not need a resurrection to supply this want. Indeed, if there were a resurrection in the future, what would happen to the temporary ethereal body which existed between physical death and the resurrection of the physical body? We begin to accumulate too many bodies!

What Does Scientific Evidence Prove?

One must be careful about the conclusions one draws from the kind of evidence presented above. The critic's argument proceeds by showing that the mind and body develop, function, and are affected correlatively. But the most that this proves, the dualist could reply — and I believe rightly — is that there exists a causal relation between certain physical states and certain mental states. It does not prove that the body is a necessary condition for the *existence* of the mind or soul. It shows that physical changes in the body can result in corresponding alterations in the abilities, content, or states of the mind, but it does not conclusively demonstrate that the mind or soul can neither exist nor function apart from the body.

To prove conclusively that the body is a necessary condition for the existence of the mind or soul, one would have to show that there is no consciousness where there is no living, physical organism. But this is notoriously difficult, if not impossible. Suppose that someone said that when his friend died, there was no consciousness or person left alive. What evidence could he adduce for such a claim? Presumably he would contend that he could no longer talk or communicate with him, that no further information came about him, or that the dead body gave no response indicative of being conscious. But this evidence or lack of evidence is ambiguous because it can be accounted

63

for by two very different hypotheses. It is true that it could be explained by the claim that the friend or his soul no longer exists, that
the demise of the physiological means a corresponding demise of the
conscious person. But it could likewise be explained by the hypothesis
that, since the body is necessary for interpersonal communication, the
friend has no way of communicating with him. Since bodily activity is
required for expressing consciousness, and since the body is dead and
no longer functioning in appropriate ways, the reason there is no
semblance of consciousness or personhood is the condition of the
body. Since this evidence can be accounted for by either hypothesis,
it does not constitute definitive evidence demonstrating that the soul
needs a body in order to exist (though it might indicate that it needs
such to communicate with embodied human beings). It simply shows
that the person is no longer certifiable by our ordinary perceptual
apparatus. What is needed here is an extension of one's powers so as
to be able to check all possible states of consciousness subsequent to
death, something which on the face of it is impossible, for one could
always claim that not all the possibilities have been covered in this
exploration for disembodied consciousness.

How, then, are we to decide the issue of whether the physical is a
necessary condition for the existence of the mental? Perhaps it must
be admitted from the outset that the problem is not capable of a
definitive solution; no conclusive proof seems available. However,
this should not dampen our investigative spirits. What we said in the
first chapter about proof might be profitably recalled. Proof yielding
absolute certainty is rarely achieved; most of our knowledge proceeds
in terms of degrees of probability, determined according to the nature
of the subject matter and type of evidence conceivably available.

Granted this, we might approach our question by asking why we
should adopt the one hypothesis (that there is merely a causal relation
between certain physical processes and certain mental states, but that
the mind can exist and function independently of the body) rather
than the other (that the physical is a necessary condition for the
existence and functioning of the mental). The evidence for the latter
hypothesis is the extensive correlation which we have just noted
between physical processes and mental states; this along with similar
evidence suggests the strong probability that the physical is requisite
to the mental. If he is to attack this probabilistic evidence, the dualist
must do much more than criticize its failure to produce demonstrative

certitude; he must present convincing evidence or arguments to the contrary. Two sorts of arguments are frequently presented.

The first was developed in detail in chapter three. There we noted that man is unique from all other creatures in that he alone has the power of conceptual thought. That is, only he can think by forming and using abstract ideas or concepts. Further, we noted that concepts are universals: they extend over and include the totality of things which might be subsumed under a certain class. For example, the concept of an oak tree includes all individual oak trees, past, present, or future, actual or possible. It does not denote any one particular tree standing in a certain place. But nothing that exists physically is universal; everything that exists as a physical object (in the physical mode of existence) is particular. The tree we see, the orange we smell, the bird we hear, the cat we touch, the cherry pie we taste, are all individual things. (A) Therefore, concepts do not exist in the physical mode of existence. They are not physical but immaterial. As immaterial, they cannot be the object of or embodied in a physical organ, like the brain. (B) Therefore, that which works with or knows concepts must be an immaterial thing, and this is called the mind or soul.

Though the argument appears to be sound, there is in conclusion A a fatal ambiguity. Conclusion A can be understood in two senses. On the one hand, the conclusion that concepts do not exist in the physical mode of existence might be interpreted as stating that concepts are not physical things, where the emphasis is placed on denying to them a particular mode of existence. Understood in this fashion, the conclusion does not affirm any particular mode of their existence. That is, this denial that they possess physical or material existence is not equivalent to the assertion that they possess immaterial existence. This can be seen in that statement A so interpreted is compatible with the denial to concepts of *both* immaterial and material modes of existence. In short, all that is stated by conclusion A is that concepts are not physical things, that they do not have a physical or material existence. But if the conclusion be understood in this sense, then the second conclusion (B) — that the mind is an immaterial thing — does not follow. For since nothing is affirmed about the mode of existence of concepts, nothing can be concluded about the mode of existence of that which works with or knows concepts. Thus, conclusion A cannot be used as a premise in an argument to support conclusion B, that there exists a non-physical soul entity.

If, on the other hand, conclusion A be taken to mean that concepts are not physical things, but *immaterial things*, then that the mind is non-physical or immaterial follows. But in this case the first conclusion appears to be a meaningless statement. Consider the statement as a response to the question, Are concepts physical things or non-physical things? The question, it seems, does not make sense, just as it does not make sense to inquire whether time is a physical or non-physical thing or whether justice is a physical or non-physical thing. Concepts, time, and justice are not that sort of thing. It is like asking, What size is green? It is true that one can inquire about the mode of existence of such things as tables, chairs, trees, houses, angels, or God, and it is true that these words and words like "time," "justice," and "concept" are nouns. But though the question can be asked meaningfully with respect to some nouns, it does not follow that it is a meaningful question with respect to all. The arguer, it seems, has been misled by similarities of grammar into thinking that the same question is meaningful in both types of cases. But clearly it is not. Accordingly, interpreted in this second sense, conclusion B follows, but conclusion A is a meaningless statement. In short, the argument succumbs to a serious dilemma: either conclusion A is meaningless, or if meaningful, conclusion B, establishing the soul or mind as an immaterial entity, does not follow necessarily from A.

A second argument for the claim that the soul can exist and function apart from the body relates more directly to the question of immortality. It is claimed that spiritual and psychical phenomena provide evidence for the post-mortem existence of the individual soul. For our purposes these kinds of experiences may be divided into two types: those in which the deceased individual is himself perceived by our senses, and those where special communications come through the use of paranormal powers.

The first category has had a special place in the history of Christianity, particularly in but not restricted to the mystical tradition. The Scriptures recount that Moses and Elijah appeared to the disciples on the Mount of Transfiguration, and that Samuel appeared to King Saul before his death. Similarly there are numerous accounts of appearances of the Virgin, at points as disparate as Lourdes, France, and Guadalupe, Mexico. Perhaps the most systematic and detailed accounts of appearances, however, can be found in the mystic literature, with its extensive reports of visions, locutions, and other sensory experiences.

I do not intend here to broach the issue of the validity or invalidity of such claims. Even if we grant their validity, it is interesting and important to note that the visual appearances of such individuals — saints or commoners — subsequent to their deaths are always of a person in some recognizable, bodily form. But what about instances of voices and locutions? Does not this provide the necessary evidence? I think not. They either provide no evidence at all, for we have no way of knowing whether the person speaking is embodied or not, or indicate that the person has a body, since the only mode of verbal communication known to us is by means of physical organs, such as the larynx.

Evidence from the second category, which involves paranormal powers, is likewise inconclusive. The thrust of the argument is that information supposedly not known to the living is received or made available to them. Its source must therefore not be the living, but disembodied persons. However, as Antony Flew has argued, not only are there parallel phenomena which have been interpreted non-spiritualistically, but by wielding Occam's razor we can account for these phenomena by appealing to nothing more than the paranormal powers of the "receivers" or mediums themselves.[6] To account for these phenomena requires the presence and activity of paranormal powers such as telepathy, even if one also appeals to the existence of disembodied spirits as the source of the information. But if we can explain the phenomena by these powers alone, the source of the information being living beings, then there is no need to appeal to disembodied spirits. Consequently, neither spiritual appearances nor paranormal communication is sufficient to establish good reason for believing in the existence of disembodied souls.

What can we conclude from this? I believe we can state that, though there is no evidence to *conclusively* or *demonstrably* establish that bodies are or are not necessary conditions for the existence of souls or minds, it seems most reasonable, in light of the great amount of scientific evidence, to believe that the body, particularly the brain and the central nervous system, is necessary for the existence and functioning of the mind. The dualist's arguments, at least the ones considered above, have not succeeded in providing adequate, contrary evidence which would overthrow that presented by the critic.

Of course, the dualist can modify his account in such a way as to hold that the body is a necessary condition for the mental. That is, he can maintain that man is a combination of body and soul, each constituting a necessary part of the whole person. However, if he does this, he can no longer appeal to the traditional reasoning, developed in chapter three, to show that man can be immortal, for there is now no subsistent, self-conscious, personal being aware of its past which does not die. Neither can he maintain, assuming man to be immortal, that a conscious being persists between the death and re-creation of the body. Either there is no such intermediate state or else the soul entity persists in an unconscious state for a period of time until it is reunited with its re-created body. The latter seems clearly unacceptable, for it conflicts with the characterization of the soul as the ground of consciousness, as well as with the arguments which are usually given to prove the existence of such an entity. If the former is the case, then either the re-creation of the body occurs immediately upon death (which conflicts with the affirmations noted earlier in this chapter that re-creation of the body is a future event) or else the soul ceases to exist along with the body until both are re-created (for which act of annihilation there is no corroborating evidence). In short, though there are ways out of the difficulties posed by the apparent necessity of the body for acts of thinking and consciousness, none of the options thereby provided seems acceptable.

Completing the Tale

Furthermore, whichever position the dualist ultimately adopts — whether he maintains that the body is not necessary for the existence or functioning of the mind, though physical processes can and do causally affect mental states, or whether he holds that the physical is a necessary (but not a sufficient) condition for the existence and function of the mind — one would expect that the dualist could and would provide a reasonable and adequate account of the causal connection between the physical and the mental. But his failure to do so constitutes our third criticism of the dualist position.

For the dualist the soul is non-physical, non-spatial, unextended; the body is physical, spatial, extended. The soul does affect the body, for my thought of moving my arm can be translated into the appropriate muscular response. Similarly the body can affect the soul, for the sensuous appearance of the type on this page arouses in me conceptual realization of its contents. But if these two entities are so disparate in nature, how can they interact with each other; in what way and by what means can the one influence the other? The relationship cannot be physical, for the soul is not physical. Neither can it be spiritual, for the body is physical, not spiritual. The problem here is not whether they interact; that they do is obvious. Rather, it is encumbent upon the dualist to present a reasonable and persuasive explanation which accounts for such interactions. And none has been forthcoming.

Obviously, the fact that the dualist's story has not yet been completed (by the provision of the description of the manner of interaction between body and soul) does not disprove the tale. However, it does suggest that if we are to adopt this view of man, answers to this question must be forthcoming.

Problem of Meaning

There is a fourth objection which has achieved prominence in recent thought. Its major contention is that the dualist account of the soul or mind is ultimately meaningless. Let us see how this is developed.

Dualism urges that the soul in and of itself is capable of such activities as understanding, willing, and thinking. After it divests itself of the physical body in death, it continues to be not only self-conscious, but also able to know certain truths and will certain things. Accordingly, it claims that the statements "The soul (mind) thinks" or "The soul (mind) wills" are meaningful. Indeed, one can substitute a large number of mental processes here for "think" and "will," for example, "believe," "remember," "doubt," or "wish."

But what does it *mean* to say that the soul (mind) wills or the soul (mind) thinks? The dualist cannot contend that words such as "will" or "think" get their meaning from a public, bodily performance, for these processes can occur without the presence of a body.[7] If they derived their meaning from public performance, the dualist could not meaningfully say that the disembodied soul (mind) thinks. Rather, it seems that the dualist believes that mental process words derive their meaning from some private experience that we have. What I mean by "think," for example, derives from introspective awareness of what I do psychologically when I perform the activity of thinking. I observe a particular process going on in my mind and label that process "thinking." I then remember it, such that when it again occurs, it is obvious to me that it is the same process which before I labeled "thinking." In this manner I fix my attention on certain inner processes, and connect them with mental process words like "think," "will," "believe," "doubt," and "remember." As such, words such as "will" and "think" *stand for* or *mean* some private experience that we have. When, for example, I say that I am thinking that the train arrives at five o'clock, what I *mean* by "think" is some sort of mental or psychical process going on within my head, whose object or content is the idea of the train's arrival. Similarly, "will" means to perform some sort of internal volitional activity.

Further, since thinking and willing are non-physical events occurring within me, these experiences are accessible only to me. No one else can have access to or witness my act of thinking. Another might infer from my bodily movements or from my responses to his queries that I am thinking, or more specifically, about what I am thinking, but this, at best, is an inference based upon his own experience of his private thoughts and their bodily manifestation.

Consequently, since the meaning of mental action words is an internal psychical process, and since this process is a private, uncheckable performance occurring within and known only to me, the meaning of these words must likewise be private. As such, we are faced with a private language regarding our mental performance words. A private language is one in which the words refer only to one's own private experiences, such that only the speaker knows and is in a position to know the meaning of the terms that he uses. Each individual finds himself enclosed in his own language world, unable to communicate adequately the meaning of his terms to others, or to understand the private meaning of the language used by others.

The following example might help clarify this. When I say that I am thinking, only I know what the word "thinking" means, for only I have access to the activity to which it refers. Since you cannot directly be aware of my internal activity of thinking, you cannot really know what *I* mean by "think." Of course, you use the same mark or symbol, but in your case you use it to refer to your own private process. When you hear me say that I was thinking about the five o'clock train, you must interpret the word "think" in terms of your internal, mental activity. But how do I know that the activity which you refer to by "think" is the same as the activity to which I refer by the same symbol? Since both activities are private, we have no way of knowing. We have constructed for ourselves a private language referring to private mental processes.

But there are severe difficulties to be found in a doctrine of meaning which necessitates private language. First of all, in a private language one can make no distinction between having used a particular word, such as "know," consistently and *seeming* to have used the word consistently, and hence correctly.[8] For example, yesterday I used the word "know" to refer to a particular kind of mental act, say one with a certain tingle. Today I think I used the word "know" for that same sort of activity with a tingle. But I have no way of knowing whether I have used "know" for the same activity in both cases, accompanied by the same kind of tingle. I might have; I seem to have done so; but I cannot be sure. Moreover I have no way to ascertain or check if I am using it consistently. There is no standard of meaning outside my subjective impression that I think I am using it consistently. Hence, the distinction between consistent and seemingly consistent usage has disappeared. But if this distinction disappears, so must also disappear the concept of correct usage, which depends upon this distinction.

Similarly with rules, for to use a word consistently is to follow a rule. In a private language there appears to be no difference between following a rule and seeming to follow a rule (or being under the impression that one is following a rule).[9] What is the evidence that I am really following a rule rather than *apparently* following one? The proof that I am following a rule cannot come from another impression, for I could be as mistaken about the impression to which I am comparing the impression in question as I am about the impression in question itself. To prove that I am consistently following a rule, I must compare my impression of following a rule with something independent of my impression. But the very nature of a private language prevents this, for there is no standard of meaning outside my own impression that I am following a rule. The meanings of my language are determined by and known to me alone. Consequently, my private language cannot have any rules.

But is a language without rules and without correct usage a language at all? If any word can apply, consistently or inconsistently, to anything, can we say we have a language? Private language is, in reality, no language at all. Hence, if we adopt the view of meaning which seems to be suggested by the dualistic view of man — that mental-performance words get their meaning from private, uncheckable experiences and from those experiences alone — we are forced into saying that our language about the soul is a private language, and ultimately that it is not a language at all. As such, we cannot communicate to others or even ourselves understand what we mean when we make certain statements about the soul or mind. Language about the soul appears to be meaningless.

Contrary to this view, our words derive their meaning from their use in the public world. Mental process words get their meaning, first of all, from their application to human beings *as a whole.* That is, they refer to the activity of a psycho-physical organism in the physical world. For example, understanding involves not merely psychical processes, but also the performance of certain physical activities. It might be the vocalization of counting the scores of a tennis match, the threading of a bobbin on a sewing machine, or the maneuvering of a car into a narrow parking place. In each case the entire organism is involved. It could not be said that I understand how to park a car if all that occurred was a private, psychical process without the actual, physical maneuvering of an auto once, or more likely several times, into a parking place without ramming the vehicles in front of or behind me. It is the conjunction of psychical and physical which allows me to say that I understand. Consequently, we do not know what it would be like or what it would mean to (univocally) apply such concepts as thinking, willing, and understanding to a disembodied, non-physical, or immaterial being like the soul.

Secondly, terms such as "think" and "will" are also given meaning in terms of their connection with physical characteristics of our environment and the observable behavior of people who think and will. To say that I am in a particular mental state is to affirm, among other things, that I am in any of a large collection of publicly observable situations and that I am doing or am disposed to do one of a number of observable performances. For example, to say that I understand is not to report some private mental experience of understanding, such that I am forming a picture in my mind of what I understand, or some such activity. What is determinative of whether I understand a particular bit of material is whether I can publicly explain the concept or repeat the specified operation by myself. To understand, for example, how to keep score in tennis is to be able to perform the actual scoring operations for a game. If the individual who claims to understand scores it as he would a football game, he does not understand; if he performs the scoring properly on his own, then he understands. Understanding does not solely signify a private mental phenomenon, but also a nexus of behavioral activities which the individual who understands either can or does perform. This performance occurs in the public world, with other people in a physical environment. Thus, mental terms also derive their meaning from the public, physical context in which they are used.

Since these predicates derive their meaning from public behavior in a physical environment, the application of these terms strictly to private psychical processes of the soul would be meaningless. To say that a soul thinks or wills, either we would have to use the terms in the same way that they are used in our present experience — which is shown to be impossible because our present experience is a public, embodied one in a physical environment — or we would have to give these predicates entirely new meanings, which leads to scepticism (for we have no basis or experience from which to form these meanings) and to the problems of a private language as seen above. This is not to deny that we have private psychical experiences such as thinking and willing. It is simply to say that from the reality of private, psychical experiences we cannot conclude that words which supposedly refer to them derive their meaning *solely* from such occult or private activities.

This same problem arises when we say that the soul is the true self or the real person. By "self" the dualist refers to some inner, private entity which only he can experience. Others cannot know my self except by inference from my bodily actions or words. But if used in this way, the term "self" becomes a member of my private language which only I can understand, and thus subject to all the difficulties associated with private languages.

What we mean by "self" is not some inner substance, necessarily private; it is not some sort of mysterious entity that only I have access to, but that others can never know except indirectly, insofar as they infer what my self is like from my bodily behavior. Rather, my self is tied to all sorts of non-psychological traits and characteristics. Persons and selves depend on embodied external modes of life in a physical environment, such that one cannot know what the self is apart from bodily activities.

> . . . unless there were a common life which people share, which they were taught and came to learn, there could be no notion of a person. To call these common activities a façade, an outer show, and to contrast

them with a logically private reality is a mistake, since without these activities there could be neither reality nor façade. . . . The public is the precondition of the private, not a construct of it. This being so, what it means to be a person cannot be divorced or abstracted from these common features of human life.

Thus, any attempt to say that the essence of the self is thought, and that this thinking self is best depicted as an inner substance, never directly knowable, is doomed to failure. . . . The supposition, therefore, that something called a thinking substance (soul) could survive the disappearance or disconnection of these other features is fundamentally confused.[10]

The consequence of this argument is that though there might be a soul, we cannot speak meaningfully concerning its disembodied functions or activities. But such is practically fatal to the notion of the soul. As we noted above, the only way one can speak positively about the soul is in terms of its functions: thinking, self-identity, moral consciousness. But if these function-predicates are meaningless when applied solely to the activity of a non-physical soul, then there is nothing positive that we can affirm about the soul. It can be described only in a negative fashion, by saying what it is not.

It has been argued by Purtill that this objection is irrelevant to the traditional Christian position, for this view holds that the body will be re-created and reunited with the soul.[11] The body and soul together constitute the self. Thus, the term "self" and mental activity terms which involve some form of life activity can be used in describing life after death.

However, though this is true regarding the embodied state which is to occur after re-creation of the body, it still fails to dispense with the difficulty of the intermediate state. Traditional Christian views hold that the self exists and that there is mental activity during this time. Yet if mental activity involves some form of life activity, we cannot predicate mental activity terms of disembodied souls. Neither can we call disembodied souls "selves." Thus, either during this time the soul is not a self and inactive and contentless (which then, among other things, makes it impossible for the dualist to appeal to the considerations developed in the previous chapter regarding the possibility of immortality) or else the original difficulty developed above recurs.

In conclusion, though there might exist such an entity as a soul, the dualist is faced with great difficulty in speaking meaningfully about it, in describing it and its functions. For to do so involves him in the construction of a private language, where the terms used derive their meaning from private experiences. But private languages seem to be no language at all. Thus, to give meaning to this term "soul" becomes a primary requisite of the dualistic thesis.

The Spiritual in Man

But, some still might object, can one surrender the concept of the soul without at the same time sacrificing the spiritual dynamic or dimension of man? Is not this notion essential to Christian theology?

The concept of the soul is required to explain this dimension of man only if one persists in thinking in substantive terms. Traditional philosophy and theology have had a penchant for reification, for taking abstract terms and postulating their existence as real objects in the world. For example, language about space in the seventeenth and eighteenth centuries conjured up in men's minds the idea of an absolute receptacle, a divine sensorium, in which all things were located. Space was a thing rather than a relationship between things. Similarly with the spiritual dimension or aspect of man (often termed his *imago dei* or image of God). Some who have retained the usage of these concepts frequently either reify them or locate them in some kind of entity which is unextended, non-spatial, and non-sensible. Without such an entity, they argue, man has lost his spiritual dimension.

But the spiritual dimension of man is not intrinsically dependent upon the existence of such an elusive entity. It is not to be found in

> any static impression on man's being, but in his responsibility towards his Creator. In the Genesis account of creation God, when He creates man, is regarded as taking up an attitude of deeper personal concern for him (Genesis 1:26) and an approach that involves Himself in a closer relationship with man His creature than with the rest of creation. . . . Man is made to respond to God's gracious word in personal love and trust. Only in this response can man be what he truly is.[12]

Man's spiritual dimension has to do with his *relationship* to God and his fellowmen, a relationship which has been severed through the self-assertive activity of the person.[13] It is a relationship of love, forgiveness, trust, obedience, giving, faith, and hope. But this relationship and the development of these qualities is no consequence of the possession of some sort of spiritual entity; rather, the relationship and disrelationship are features of the whole man. Love, trust, obedience are actions that I do with my body as much as with my mind. Indeed, their manifestation cannot be isolated in any one part of my being; they are activities of my entire being-in-the-world.

If the only reason for persisting in a belief in the existence of a human soul is to "protect" the spiritual dimension of man, then it might be healthy to allow the term to drop from our religious vocabulary. Such a move, far from destroying faith in the spiritual aspect of man, will aid in clarifying precisely where the spiritual lies: it lies not in the possession of an entity, but in the style of life one leads insofar as it manifests a relation to God and to one's fellowman. To be a Christian is to live from the perspective that the living Christ indwells oneself, that he controls one's thoughts and actions, and that actions manifesting love of my neighbor and love for myself flow from this perspective. Far from removing the spiritual dimension, the elimination of "soul" frees man to be concerned as a *whole person* with living the Christian life.

But if we abandon the concept of a soul entity, will we not have forfeited our only rational grounds for belief in individual life after death? This question, I suspect, reveals the ultimate source of the doctrine of the soul entity. The concept of a soul was introduced in order to provide for and guarantee the possibility of life after death for the individual. If there is a part of man which does not die, death is not so much of a risk. To answer this question, we must turn to the other analysis of the nature of man indicated in chapter two, monism.

NOTES

1. I Corinthians 15:3-4, 12-22, 51-54.

2. Richard L. Purtill, "The Intelligibility of Disembodied Survival," *Christian Scholar's Review*, V, No. 1 (1975), 7.

3. Antony Flew, *A New Approach to Psychical Research* (London: C.A. Watts & Co., 1953), p. 76.

4. The means by which a soul in a disembodied state can acquire new thoughts or experiences, or can relate to other finite individuals or God is, of course, problematic. It is conceivable, though, that new experiences or knowledge are derived by means of extra-sensory perception, intuition, and

clairvoyance, and that communication between persons takes place by means of mental telepathy.

5. *The Republic,* X, 614d-615a.

6. Flew, *op. cit.,* ch. 7.

7. Unfortunately, those who raise this objection frequently fail to distinguish between the perceptual and conceptual activities of the individual. Consequently, they couch their objection in terms of seeing, feeling, and hearing. But dualists, particularly Christian dualists, have long held that the perceptual activities need the presence of the body. The disembodied soul cannot perform these perceptual functions. Hence, their objection in terms of perceptual performances completely misses the mark. Accordingly, I have reformulated their objection in terms of conceptual activities, which the dualist does maintain can be performed by a disembodied soul. See P.T. Geach, *God and the Soul* (N.Y.: Schocken Books, 1969), pp. 19ff; D.Z. Phillips, *Death and Immortality* (N.Y.: St. Martin's Press, 1970), pp. 4ff.

8. Ludwig Wittgenstein, *Philosophical Investigations* (N.Y.: Macmillan, 1953), par. 258.

9. *Ibid.,* par. 259.

10. Phillips, *op. cit.,* pp. 5-6.

11. Purtill, *op. cit.,* pp. 8-10.

12. "Man," *The New Bible Dictionary,* ed. J.D. Douglas (Grand Rapids: Eerdmans, 1962), p. 776.

13. Ephesians 4:24-25.

CHAPTER FIVE

Monism and Immortality

At THIS POINT IT MIGHT BE HELPFUL TO PAUSE BRIEFLY TO
review what we have accomplished thus far. We have defined immortality as the actual existence of the individual human person for an
indefinite period subsequent to his death, with that which makes for
his own personal identity and the awareness of this self-identity essentially intact. Further, we have suggested that the problem of human
immortality is in reality two problems. First, "What must man be like
in order for there to be the possibility that he could live subsequent to
his death?" and secondly, "What good reasons can be given for maintaining a belief in life after death?" In order to answer the first question, it was necessary to explore various views of the nature of man.
These contending views were grouped under two classifications:
dualism (or pluralism), in which the individual is composed of elements of different kinds, including an immaterial part called the mind
or soul; and monism, in which the individual is a psycho-physical
unity.

In the third chapter we undertook to explore the dualistic view
and what it means to say that man has a soul. On the basis of our study
of the nature of the soul, we concluded that man, understood in this
fashion, was capable of being immortal. When the individual "died,"
his physical body died; but since his true person — his soul — was
non-physical, it was not subject to death and hence could continue to
exist. However, in chapter four we noted that there are serious difficulties confronting this position. Its denial of the death of the real
person contradicts our ordinary way of speaking about death; it seems
to conflict with science's conclusion that the body is a necessary
condition for the existence of mental processes; it fails to inform us
how the mind and body can and do interact with and influence each

other; its language about the soul appears to involve the appeal to the philosophically untenable theory of private language.

The weight of these difficulties has been such as to suggest to some that we must abandon a pluralistic analysis of man and instead understand man as being a psycho-physical unity. But what does it mean to say that man is a psycho-physical unity? And how does this view account for and interpret human mental processes? Is immortality possible if one adopts this position? It is the answers to these questions which will occupy our attention in this chapter.

Behaviorism

The view of man which stands opposed to the dualistic thesis is usually termed monism. Those who maintain this position reject the supposed existence of a spiritual soul or mind which, though functioning within a body structured and operated according to natural laws, cannot be described in terms of the concepts employed by physical scientists. Man is a physical organism, such that all of his functions and operations — mental as well as bodily — are ultimately physiological events or behavioral acts.

The monistic theory has appeared in a number of guises throughout the course of Western thought. In the present century, two interpretations have had wide appeal. One of these, Behaviorism, was originally developed by the psychologist J.B. Watson. Traditional psychology considered itself to be a science of consciousness or of the mind. Accordingly, the bodily or physical aspect of man was largely neglected in its studies. As a science of mind, psychology proceeded by introspection. The psychologist or philosopher reflectively observed the contents of his own consciousness, presumably in a detached, critical, objective manner, so as to understand the nature of mental processes. Behaviorism, however, rejected these arm-chair, introspective procedures on the grounds that they introduced a subjective element into psychology. The phenomena so reported could not be observed and confirmed by independent observers, as was the case in other natural sciences. The obvious consequence of this lack of objective checking procedures was the great variety of introspective accounts and interpretations of human mental processes. To be a science, all subjectivity had to be rigorously excluded. Since Behaviorism desired to develop a scientific account of man, it replaced the methodology of an introspective account of consciousness with an objective account of human and animal behavior.

Behaviorism, however, went beyond mere methodological concerns to proffer a view of man himself. It claimed that mentalistic concepts such as "mind," "thinking," and "consciousness" had no place in an objective, scientific account, for they presupposed an outmoded and unscientific mentalistic philosophy. How then were mental phenomena to be understood? Since there is no soul but only the physical organism, mental concepts were to be redefined or analyzed in terms of objectively observable behavior. As such, what was once considered to be distinctively mental was now reduced to or seen to be nothing but behavioral responses of the organism as it interacted with its physical environment.

For example, thinking and imagery are not internal, subjective mental processes; they are not activities of a spiritual mind or soul. They are human behavioral activities. Watson equated them with faint reinstatements of certain muscular responses originally involved in speech and other motor behavior. Thinking is thus a muscular response of the organism to its environment, most frequently located in the larynx. Similarly, emotions and feelings are behavioral patterns or physical responses, predominantly of the visceral and glandular systems.

But what about mental and emotional processes which seem to occur when there are no behavioral manifestations? It seems to make sense to say that John is angry even though he is so controlling himself that he is not manifesting the kind of overt behavior which is commonly characteristic of individuals whom we term angry. Also there is evidence in terms of subsequent reports or actions to show that individuals do in fact think, even though we cannot measure any movement of their larynx. Watson's response to this was to define mental and emotional processes in terms of implicit (unobservable or minutely visible) as well as explicit behavior. In all cases of thinking, he argued, even when we cannot observe movement, there are minute or implicit movements of the laryngeal muscles. Similarly with the emotions; they are implicit as well as explicit movements of the visceral and glandular systems. What is needed are more delicate and sophisticated instruments to detect these faint movements.

Some who have attempted to improve the Behaviorist model have suggested that instead of appealing to implicit or covert behavior (which is in effect an appeal to ignorance), we should introduce the notion of disposition to account for the statement, for example, that someone is angry, though he is not manifesting anger-behavior. On this view, mental processes are to be analyzed either in terms of behavioral acts of the organism, or else in terms of dispositions of the individual to behave in a certain way should certain circumstances obtain. For example, when we say that a glass vase is brittle, brittleness is to be understood as a dispositional property. It is to assert a conditional proposition about the vase: if we dropped it from a normal height on a hard surface, or if the vase were struck by a hard object, it would not dissolve or evaporate, but would shatter into many fragments. The glass vase might never be dropped or struck; it might never manifest this brittleness. Yet we can say it is brittle because it would shatter given certain circumstances. Similarly, if I am said to be envious, it means that I am disposed to act in a certain way should certain circumstances obtain. If I had enough money, I would purchase objects similar to those possessed by the one whom I envy; I would try to outdo him by lavish spending; I would attempt to wean his friends or admirers from him to myself.

However, "dispositional statements are neither reports of observed or observable states of affairs, nor yet reports of unobserved or unobservable states of affairs. They narrate no incidents."[1] "To possess a dispositional property is not to be in a particular state, or to undergo a particular change; it is to be bound or liable to be in a particular state, or to undergo a particular change, when a particular condition is realised."[2] Dispositional properties are logical constructions out of behavior. Thus, the Behaviorist thesis is maintained: "When we describe people as exercising qualities of mind, we are not referring to occult episodes of which their overt acts and utterances are effects; we are referring to those overt acts and utterances themselves."[3]

The Identity Theory

Subsequent philosophers have felt that more is needed to fully explain human conscious processes. For one thing, it is not enough to leave the analysis of mental processes simply on the level of behavior or dispositions, for explanations of this behavior or of these dispositional properties can be suggested. Just as one might explain the dispositional property of brittleness in the glass vase by noting its molecular

81

composition and the strength of the bond between the particles (that is, by noting its physical properties), so too one might explain the behavior or disposition to behave by appeal to certain physical properties. The dispositional property of brittleness is explained by the physical state of the glass; likewise the disposition to behave in a certain way can be explained by the physical state of the organism. It is this state which causes or brings about the behavioral manifestations of the disposition. As such, an analysis of man in terms of behavior and dispositions to behave does not go far enough.

Secondly, related to what we have just said, the mental appears to have a genuinely causal explanatory role. We might say that John acted the way he did at the party *because* he was envious. But an analysis in terms of dispositions eliminates this apparently causal explanatory aspect of the mental, for if envy as a disposition is a mere logical construction out of envy-behavior, we cannot rightly say that it caused an action.

Thirdly, the reports of mental processes going on inside me, of which I am immediately aware, appear to be *genuine* reports of real processes.

> When I think, but my thoughts do not issue in any action, it seems obvious as anything is obvious that something is going on inside me which constitutes my thought. It is not simply that I would speak or act if some conditions were to be fulfilled. Something is going on, in the strongest and most literal sense of "going on," and this something is my thought. Rylean Behaviorism denies this, and so it is unsatisfactory as a theory of mind.[4]

My behavior is not identical with my thought, as Behaviorism claims, but is rather the expression of my thought.

Rejecting Behaviorism as a not completely satisfactory theory, while at the same time refusing to opt for a dualist view of man, recent monists have developed what is termed the Identity or Central-State Materialist Theory of the mind. The Identity Theory contends that insofar as a statement about a mental state or sensation is a report of something, that something is in fact a brain process, brain state, or a process within the central nervous system.[5]

This must not be understood to mean that "thought" means the same as "brain process of a certain sort." Statements about thoughts and sensations cannot be translated into nor are synonymous with statements about brain processes. Neither does it mean that statements about sensations and thoughts can be reduced to or analyzed into statements about states of the brain. It is *not* a theory about the meaning of mental terms or concepts at all, but rather about a logical identification which, if true, can ultimately be subject to empirical verification.

Neither do the proponents of the Identity Theory deny the existence or reality of mental or psychical states such as perceiving, conceiving, remembering, and imagining; mental states are as real as those physical processes which can be objectively observed. However, the event which the mental language reports is ultimately the same as or identical with the event which would be reported by the neurologist. What they deny is that states of consciousness are irreducibly psychical. Using thinking as an example, the event is one and physiological — an electro-chemical transference in the brain — though the perspectives from which the event is reported (as a mental state or as a process of the central nervous system) and the language used to report these perspectives (language about minds, thinking, and concepts, and language about brain waves, synapses, and electrochemical discharges) are two. Reports based on both of the perspectives are genuine; both of the languages used are legitimate; but both refer to one and only one physical event, for thinking is a brain process.

Perhaps one of their favorite illustrations will be of help.[6] The event of lightning can be reported from two different perspectives, using different language games or systems. The physicist reports a concentrated electrical discharge occurring at a particular time and place in the atmosphere; the ordinary observer reports a bright flash of light, jaggedly etched across the stormy sky. Both of these reports are genuine and use different and non-interchangeable language; but the event they report is one and the same. Similarly, the neurologist reports electro-chemical processes within the brain, whereas the individual states that at that time he was thinking about last winter's vacation in Peru. Both of these report real events. The one uses language about synapses, neurons, and electro-chemical discharges in the brain; the other uses language about minds, ideas, concepts, and memories. Further, these two languages are logically independent, containing non-interchangeable elements. However, the events reported by these two language systems are not two different events; they both report the same event.

In short, on this view man is *in toto* a physical organism: he possesses no non-physical entity. Man does have mental experiences, but his reports of them do not refer to separate and unique events, over and above certain physical processes of the organism.

Why should one opt for this view? Those who do so readily admit their materialistic bias. But it is not a bias without support. Recent advances in neurophysiology (developing plausible electro-chemical accounts of the workings of the brain) and in molecular biology (discovering the physical and chemical mechanisms which lie at the basis of all life) provide good reasons for opting for this view of man. But not only does this metaphysical view grow out of scientific advances, it also has the advantage of potentially being empirically verifiable. If and once we establish what the logical criteria are for "deciding whether two sets of correlated observations refer to the same event or to two separate but causally related events,"[7] then it becomes a matter of empirical and scientific research to discover whether or not there is a physiological process which satisfies these logical criteria. It is this consonance with the methods and results of science, and the possibility of empirical verification which it allows, which makes this metaphysical view of man philosophically attractive.

The Question of Immortality

But if we understand man's nature in this fashion, is human immortality possible? Traditionally, those who have maintained this view of man have held that it is not possible. Man is a physical organism who dies when his body ceases to function in certain significant ways. Nothing remains in or of man which would allow him to witness his own funeral.

Moreover, it is this view of the nature of man which is most frequently presupposed by critics of the doctrine of personal life after death. Arguing from this perspective, they contend that arguments for immortality are useless because life after death is impossible.

However, this position can be challenged; even if one grants a monistic view of the nature of human beings, I think it can be shown that personal immortality is possible. It is true that, since the individual is identical with that physiological organism which ceases to function at death, he likewise ceases to exist. However, life after death is possible because, first of all, it is not self-contradictory that an individual could be physically re-created or reconstructed to possess all of the physical characteristics of the deceased, such that he would look identical to the person who died. And since consciousness is a brain process, his brain could be so re-created and programmed as to have neural and chemical components and structures identical to the deceased, such that he would have the same memories, ideas, perspectives, and personality traits as the individual who died. In short, a person precisely identical to the deceased could be re-created, with the result that the person re-created would be the same person as the one who died; he would begin again to live where the deceased left off.

This is possible, secondly, because God is omnipotent; that is, he can perform any action which does not entail a self-contradiction. Since the re-creation of the same individual is not self-contradictory, he can re-create the very same individual to begin to live at the point where death brought an end to his experience, at a time and place of God's own choosing.

In short, life after death is possible for man, even if he be interpreted in a monistic fashion. Since man is viewed as being ultimately a physiological entity, such that all his behavior can be traced back to physiological events, it is perfectly possible, and not self-contradictory, for him to be re-created physiologically identical to his past constitution and to be reprogrammed to precisely the same level of experience and intellect that he had at his death or even prior to his death. In this fashion the one who died can now live again, by the creative power of an omnipotent God.

Objections

Several objections might be raised at this point. First, it might be objected that this must mean that the deceased will be in a state of unconsciousness for a certain period of time. The answer to this must be negative. In order for an individual to be unconscious, there must exist a person who can be unconscious. But after death and prior to re-creation, there is no such person. Thus, the individual who dies will not be unconscious for a period of time (or to put it in more theological terms, there is no soul-sleep involved, for there is no sleeper). The next moment of consciousness for the person who dies will occur at the time of his re-creation and reprogramming.

But would not the deceased be aware of a time lapse between death and re-creation? Here again, the answer must be no. As in the case of non-dreaming sleep, where we are not conscious of time passing, so here too, where there is no consciousness during the intervening time between death and re-creation, there can be no consciousness of a time lapse. Re-creation, to the person re-created, will appear to take place at the next moment after death, though speaking in terms of objective measurement of time, it might be any number of years or eons later.

The point just made rests on a distinction which we frequently make, that is, between subjective time and objective time. Suppose that you are sitting in an idling car in a "No Parking or Standing" zone, waiting for your son to come out of the post office after mailing a package. You sweat a little, maintain constant alertness for a prowling police car, and glance anxiously at the post office door. It seems like it is taking forever for him to mail the package. When he finally comes out and gets into the car, you inquire, "What took you so long?" Puzzled, he turns and says, "What do you mean? It only took three minutes." The point of contrast is between two kinds of time: objective time as measured by standard reference to certain celestial movements, and subjective time as measured in terms of an individual's subjective experience.

Applying this to the time of re-creation, measured in terms of objective time, the temporal gap between an individual's death and his re-creation might be thousands, even millions, of years. However, measured in terms of subjective time, that is, in terms of the individual's own experience, the re-creation will seem to occur at the very next moment after death. The reason for this is that the deceased has had no experiences between the experiences of dying and those immediately following re-creation. The latter will seem to follow immediately upon the former. Thus, in speaking about the time of re-creation, one should make clear whether one is referring to objective time or subjective time.

Finally, and undoubtedly the most significant objection: How can the individual who is re-created be the same person as the individual who died? The person re-created will possess entirely different physical elements and will begin again to exist at a time significantly later than his death. Because he has a different composition and lacks spatio-temporal continuity, is it not nonsense to suppose that the re-created person could be identical with the deceased? To answer this objection, we must consider whether these two features are necessary conditions for all cases of personal identity.

Personal Identity

One thing we apparently do not mean by "same person" is that the individual is composed of the same material elements now as he was previously. For example, between cooking my supper last evening and frying my eggs this morning, my wife has undergone significant change. Her body cells have produced millions of new cells, and old cells which have died were washed away by her morning shower or eliminated through body waste. Indeed, if I say that she is the same person as the person I married eleven years ago, more than likely her entire physical constitution in terms of her organic cell structure has changed. One might respond that, in any case, during the time which transpired there has been a significant proportion of elements carried over from one time to the next. But this simply shows that any plausibility which this purported criterion might have initially had really derived from an application of the criterion of spatio-temporal continuity. That is, it is the continuity, not the composition, which is important.

Thus, a more likely interpretation of "same person" is in terms of continuous, spatio-temporal physical existence. My wife now is the same person that I married, either wholly or in part because it is in principle possible to trace her continuous physical existence from that wedding day until this present moment.

But is bodily continuity a necessary and/or sufficient condition for personal identity? Many have maintained that it constitutes a sufficient condition; we have tried to show in the previous chapter that this is not the case. However, the determination of whether or not it is sufficient is irrelevant to the re-creationist's case, for his view entails the absence of this condition with respect to personal life after death. That which poses a problem for him is whether spatio-temporal continuity constitutes a necessary condition for all cases of personal identity for, on his scenario, the re-created person lacks bodily continuity with the deceased. If someone cannot be identical with an individual existing at some prior time without being spatio-temporally continuous with that person, then the re-creationist's position is nonsense; the presence of a space-time gap precludes any identification.

What grounds can be adduced for the truth of the claim that bodily continuity is a necessary condition for, is part of the meaning of, personal identity? On the one hand, it would not seem to follow analytically from the concept of personal identity. Indeed, merely to stipulate this as a condition for personal identity would do little but beg the very question at issue. Further, it might be reasonably contended that re-creationism presents a relevant counter-example providing reason why this condition should not be incorporated into the definition of "personal identity."

On the other hand, ground for this might be sought in experience. But if experience be the ground, the requisite universality is absent. This is particularly the case with respect to the re-creationist's thesis, for we have had no (or relatively few) experiences with re-created individuals and therefore possess no experiential grounds from which to argue that the re-created person, though spatio-temporally discontinuous with the deceased, is not the same person. It remains possible that the re-created person provides a unique (and despoiling) case where the condition of spatio-temporal continuity does not apply.

But we need not rest our case simply on an appeal to ignorance. Our position will be strengthened if we can supply cases where we know the criterion in question to be absent, and yet continue (or would continue) to identify the person as identical with the previously encountered one. If we are successful in this, we will have shown that experience likewise fails to establish this as a criterion covering all cases.

Before considering a case involving personal identity in particular, let us first consider the identity of something which is not a person. Take, for example, a deck of cards. Generally speaking, we might agree that to predicate of this deck of cards that it is identical with a deck existing at a prior time requires that it have been spatio-temporally continuous between these times. However, let us consider the deck in the context of a *genuine* act of magic. The magician places the deck of cards into a hat, waves his magic wand, and then tilts it to the viewer, showing that the cards have disappeared. Another wave of the wand and, presto! they have returned. Note that we do not say that the deck of cards now in his hat is a new deck; rather, we affirm that it is the same deck that disappeared and was magically returned to the hat. In saying that the deck of cards *disappeared* and was magically *restored*, we indicate that neither we nor the magician nor anyone else could have traced its spatio-temporal existence between the first wave of the wand and the second. It simply disappeared. If we believed that we or he could trace its existence, or if we believed that the deck of cards now in the hat was a different deck from the first, he would not be a genuine or authentic magician but someone who was skilled in sleight of hand. Indeed, in this case it is the fact of their actual disappearance which distinguishes genuine magic from sleight of hand. In short, for this to be an instance of true magic, the restored deck must be the same deck as the original; hence spatio-temporal continuity is not a necessary condition for all cases of identity.

Two objections might be raised. First, it might be argued that this is a case involving merely an object and therefore is not relevant to personal identity. However, we could substitute Howard Cosell for the deck of cards in the above example, with identical results. The second objection is that such a case is not possible because there can be no real magic, only sleight of hand. Indeed, the necessity of spatio-temporal continuity for constituting identity is proof enough of this. Thus, to mitigate this objection we need to turn to a clearer case, one which involves *personal* identity and avoids appealing to the assumed possibility of magical acts.

For a half hour each weekday afternoon, *As the World Turns* features Bob Hughes, Lisa Coleman, and a number of other individuals. During this time they discourse on events occurring at the hospital, who of their acquaintances is having marital problems, and of the various and sundry affairs of their friends. Following the final soap commercial, they disappear until the following afternoon, when they take up living at a point in time and space related in varying degrees to that when and where the previous show ended. Their existence is one of installments encompassing numerous gaps. In this case there is no possibility of tracing their existence between yesterday and today; they did not exist during that time span. (One should be careful here not to confuse the actor — Don Hastings — who plays Bob with Bob; Don Hastings might exist between times, but not Bob Hughes.) Yet on their next appearance, we recognize and identify them as the same individuals we watched yesterday, despite their lack of spatio-temporal continuity. In such cases, bodily continuity does not appear to be a necessary condition for personal identity.

This example might be developed even further. Suppose that Don Hastings dies or takes another job, and is replaced on the production set. When the replacement appears on the screen, we are at first hesitant about acknowledging that this "new" individual is really Bob Hughes; his different physical appearance clearly indicates that he is spatio-temporally discontinuous with Bob as he appeared on Tuesday. Yet, in most cases we eventually would in fact identify the "newcomer" as Bob. And we would make this identification on the grounds that he remembers doing things that Bob previously remembered and we watched him do, manifests similar character traits, and treats other individuals and is treated by them in the same manner as the previously embodied individual. Indeed, we can clearly differentiate the case of Bob appearing with a new body from the appearance of an entirely new character, Fred.

If bodily continuity were a necessary condition of personal identity, none of this would be possible. Characters in television serials and stage plays would be different individuals after their daily or weekly gaps or fifteen minute intermissions; they could not change bodies and yet remain the same person. That these space-time gaps are possible and do in fact occur in the serials and plays shows that bodily continuity is not a necessary condition for personal identity in all cases.

It might be objected that these are not real individuals, but merely fictions created for or by us. And since they are not real individuals, they do not constitute a counter-example to the space-time continuity criterion. However, that they are not real in the sense that they do not inhabit our world — one would not expect to meet Bob Hughes in the department store or the hospital emergency ward — does not mean that they have no reality. Reality is contextual. For those reading this, individuals in television serials and theatrical productions are not real but fictitious individuals. But within the context of the television or theater production, the characters are real people, as distinguished from, say, a character in Lisa's dreams or Bob's fictitious cousin. Further, that they do not inhabit our particular reality seems quite irrelevant to whether or not they can be spoken of as having personal identity. Within their own particular context, there can be little doubt that Bob and Lisa each has a unique personal identity.

Indeed, the very reaction of the public to soap operas is an indicator of this. The characters (not the actors) are flooded with thousands of letters yearly, warning that so-and-so is out to get them, or that they should not marry so-and-so. It might be interesting to pursue what this widespread, mistaken view of the nature of their reality entails (e.g., that they are conceived to have personal identity on the level of the letter-writer), but this would take us afield. What is significant for us is the common belief that gap-inclusive people possess personal identity.

In sum, what examples of this sort show is that the absence of spatio-temporal continuity does not necessarily constitute a falsifying condition of personal identity. Of course, we have not established, nor are we trying to establish, the thesis that there is no conceivable situation in which bodily identity would be necessary. All we are asserting is that "at least one case can be consistently constructed in which bodily identity fails."[8] Thus, the re-creationist's claim that individuals can be gap-inclusive is far from nonsense.

If bodily continuity is not a condition for personal identity with respect to gap-inclusive people, what then are the conditions which determine personal identity in such cases? The re-creationist responds that, where bodily continuity is absent, physical similarity, internal states of consciousness (including conceptual categories and memories), and personality traits or patterns become highly determinative. It is true that this is still very ambiguous; we are left in the dark as to *which* physical features are necessary, *what* personality traits must be identical, *how many* memories must correspond with the deceased. However, I do not believe that it is necessary that the re-creationist solve the problem of personal identity. All he need do is to trace out the problem sufficiently so as to enable one to decide whether there are reasonable grounds for deciding whether the re-created individual is the same person as the deceased. We do not need, at this point, to determine the specifics with respect to these general features because we are not inquiring about what ways the re-created individual can be changed and still be the same person, for we have supposed that he is the same in all these respects to the deceased.

On the other hand, our task of showing re-creationism to be a reasonable and coherent doctrine is not yet complete, for the introduction of internal states of consciousness, and in particular memory, provides the basis for two other objections to the re-creationist's thesis. The first objection seeks to return to bodily continuity as a necessary condition for personal identity by contending that the appeal to memory claims presupposes this very condition, whereas the second goes further to claim that neither bodily continuity, physical similarity, nor internal states of consciousness are sufficient to establish personal identity. The decision to call someone identical with rather than merely similar to another is purely conventional. Let me consider these in turn.

Regarding the first, it is argued that one cannot affirm memory but deny bodily continuity as a necessary condition for personal identity. Use of memory claims presupposes bodily continuity of the individual both at some previous point of existence and at the present moment. Memory claims are fallible. Thus, we need some way of distinguishing between mere claims to remember past performances and the actual remembering of these performances (which is infallible). But verification of memory claims presupposes (1) previous physical (embodied) existence, and (2) continuous contemporary physical existence. Only if the person now exists physically continuous for a time can we test whether he can correctly use the term "remember," that is, whether he understands memory language. And only if the person existed for a length of time embodied can we check out claims to remember. But if this is the case, the objection proceeds, memory is not an independent standard of personal identity; it presupposes and is dependent upon bodily continuity.[9]

That the appeal to memory is dependent upon *previous*[10] continued bodily existence is, I believe, indisputable. To use an illustration from B.A.O. Williams, suppose that a man went

> to a crowded party, where he sees a girl who is like all the other girls at the party except that she has red hair. This girl sings various songs and quarrels with the band; she is easily identified on each occasion by the colour of the hair. The man later meets a platinum blonde who recalls singing songs at a party and quarreling with the band. He can identify her as the red-haired girl at the party, even though she has changed the colour of her hair in the meantime. . . . [However] if the girl had remarkably changed the colour of her hair between songs and before the quarrel, identifying her at the various stages of the party would have been more difficult, but not impossible; but if [she] had changed bodies frequently, identification would become not just difficult but impossible.[11]

In such a case, the recollection by the platinum blonde encountered later of being the singer at the party would be difficult or impossible to verify, because there was no continuously existent, embodied singer to be identified with.

However, that some sort of bodily continuity during the event remembered is required by the criterion of memory (to enable witnesses to identify the person who performed such and such a token act), does not entail that there *always* had to be bodily continuity. That is, it does not entail that the platinum blonde necessarily had continuous existence between the party and the later encounter. She might have ceased to exist immediately after the party, and was re-created prior to the second encounter. In such a case it would be (theoretically) possible both to check out her memory claims about the past, and also to now test whether she can correctly use "remember." Thus, though memory as a criterion for personal identity presupposes that at some time or other (that is, during the events which are purportedly remembered) there was or is bodily continuity on the part of the individual, this does not entail the stronger thesis that memory is dependent upon unbroken bodily continuity. Or to put it another way, this point about memory refutes the thesis which asserts that there is no conceivable situation in which bodily continuity would be necessary, though it does not refute the thesis that such continuity need not occur in every case or all the time.

The second objection is that merely to have memory claims about being the person who performed such and such actions at a previous time does not *compel* us to assert the identity of the individual who makes the memory claims with the individual whose actions are purportedly recalled. The reason for this is that "it is not logically impossible that two different persons should *claim* to remember being this man, and this is the most we can get."[12] Again taking an example suggested by Williams, suppose that two individuals, Charles and Robert, come into existence or undergo changes, and that they both claim that they remember performing actions which Guy Fawkes performed. If we grant that one individual cannot be in two places at the same time, then we cannot claim that they both are identical with Guy Fawkes. Neither can we say that one is he but the other is only like him, for we have no way of determining which is which.

> So it would be best, if anything, to say that both had mysteriously become like Guy Fawkes, clairvoyantly know about him, or something

93

like this. If this would be the best description of each of the two, why would it not be the best description of Charles if Charles alone were changed?[13]

Thus, it is concluded, memory claims are not sufficient to force us to conclude that the re-created individual is identical with rather than merely similar to the deceased. Only if there were determinable bodily continuity could we guarantee that Charles and not Robert is Guy.

This argument, of course, does not show or prove that Charles is not and cannot be Guy Fawkes. That he is Guy certainly still is logically possible. What it does seem to indicate is that there is no necessity for concluding that he really is Guy rather than that he is merely like him (similar to him in the above-described respects). We can opt for identity; but it is not logically requisite that we do so. Thus, whether or not such a person was the same is a matter of linguistic decision: it depends on whether we choose to call him the same person. This conventionality is purportedly fatal to the re-creationist's position, for he has failed to provide a criterion to ensure that the person in the after-life is identical with the deceased and not merely similar to him.[14]

In reply, it might be granted that the investigator cannot discover any specific evidence which would compel us to say that Charles is identical with rather than merely similar to Guy. There seems to be nothing contradictory involved in denying that, even with identical physical features, personality traits, and memory claims, Charles is not Guy. Thus, one might agree that what is required here is a decision on the part of the individual himself or an observer that Charles is Guy. However, to say that it is a matter of decision is *not* to say that the decision is an arbitrary one. The decision that he is the same person as Guy can be made on the ground that, not only is there no good reason not to identify him with Guy (in the case where there is only one such claimant), but there is good reason to thus identify him. Of course two people could look alike, have the same character and skills, personality and memory claims, and still be merely similar. There is no way of deducing identity from these features (though of course the greater the extent of these similarities, the greater the likelihood there is that we are dealing with the same individual and not merely a similar one). However, two people cannot have the same memories (true memory claims) about deeds performed only by one agent and still not be the same. Identity appears to be deducible from true memories. Accordingly, if one holds, as I think it is reasonable to hold, that seriously proffered memory claims about past actions are frequently (though by no means always) right, this would then give good reason to say that Charles was Guy, not merely similar to him. This, of course, does not enable us to decide the reliability of any one particular memory claim. However, where there is a large bank of claims which could be verified, it does provide good reason for claiming identity.

It is true that if there were more than one claimant with identical features, we would have no good reason to say that one rather than another is identical with the deceased, for we could not decide whose memory claims were true and whose were false. However, the re-creationist's supposition is that there will be one and only one re-created individual per deceased, and that each claimant would make memory claims concerning the solo-performance acts of each deceased respectively on a one-to-one basis. In such a situation, it would appear reasonable to claim that memory claims, in conjunction with the other features specified above, would provide good grounds for identity claims.

Application to Immortality

We can now respond to the objection that the re-creationist's thesis cannot be held to be a rationally coherent doctrine — that the re-created individual could not be the same as the deceased person. So long as the re-created person has the same or substantially similar physical, mental, and personality traits and memories to the deceased, it would seem most reasonable to conclude that he can be and probably is identical with the deceased. Further, lack of bodily continuity would not be sufficient to falsify his claim to personal identity with the deceased. Thus, even on a monistic view of the nature of man, life after death is possible.[15]

One might wonder, however, whether immortality after this fashion really is desirable. In particular, would I want to be precisely identical to the way I was at the time of my death? If I died in old age, would a future life lived in a state of decrepitude or senility be meaningful or desirable? Or if I died, afflicted with a disease accompanied by tormenting pain and irreversible debilitation, would I want to be re-created at a point where this would continue? Given these and similar considerations, would I indeed want to begin living at the point where I died?

The re-creationist, however, is not committed to a position which requires exact similarity of the re-created to the deceased in every detail. Above we noted that all that is required is that the features instantiated be substantially similar to those of the deceased. That is, the re-created person can be different in ways which do not essentially affect that person's personal identity; slight modifications of features — physical, mental, personality — do not constitute a falsifying condition of his personal identity with the deceased. For example, if my father, between the time I last saw him and the next time I see him, loses an appreciable amount of hair, gains visible inches at the belt line, or even loses one of his limbs, I could still identify him as the same individual whom I once called my father. Similarly with personality and mental traits: if he has become more forgetful or has changed his opinion about certain matters, he could still be identified by me as my father.

How much one can alter specific physical, mental, and personality traits before one loses one's personal identity is a difficult and perhaps ultimately unresolvable problem. The very quest for a critical threshold might itself be a meaningless one. What can be affirmed, however, is that some changes can occur in the re-created person without a change in personal identity occurring.

To what extent this observation allows St. Paul's affirmation in I Corinthians that the re-created body will be a spiritual, not a physical, body remains to be determined. In particular, it depends upon two things: what a "spiritual" body is, and the extent to which features can be altered before personal identity is lost. A hint as to the former is provided by the accounts of the post-resurrection appearances of Jesus. On the one hand, it is clear that he possessed new abilities and powers: he could appear and disappear at will or pass through walls unharmed. On the other hand, these new powers which he acquired apparently were not sufficient to make him a different individual from the one who was crucified. At the very least it is clear that he was physically recognizable to his disciples. Unfortunately, however, we are told next to nothing about the status of this re-created body.

The point I wish to make, despite the uncertainty surrounding these two factors, is that re-creation conceivably can result in slightly different characteristics. However, for the re-created individual to be the same person as the deceased, the former characteristics cannot be so altered that they affect one's personal identity.

Finally, one should be careful to distinguish what is possible under monism from that which is possible under a dualistic schema. Under the form of dualism discussed in chapter three, death of the person is not possible; immortality is provided for by the persistence of a soul-entity which is myself and does not die. Under monism (and the form of dualism where the complex of body and soul, not merely the soul, is the person) survival is not possible; the individual does die. What is possible is *life after death.* Thus, if one adopts a monistic view of man, one must be careful to distinguish life after death from survival (or "immortality" narrowly defined as "not-dying"); only the former is possible under this view. Hence, the monist should be guarded about his language, taking care to use "immortality" in the broad sense of "life after death."

NOTES

1. Gilbert Ryle, *The Concept of Mind* (N.Y.: Barnes and Noble, 1949), p. 125.

2. *Ibid.,* p. 43.

3. *Ibid.,* p. 25.

4. D.M. Armstrong, "The Nature of Mind," *The Mind-Brain Identity Theory,* ed. C.V. Borst (N.Y.: St. Martin's Press, 1970), p. 72.

5. J.J.C. Smart, "Sensations and Brain Processes," *The Philosophical Review,* LXVIII (1959); reprinted in Borst, *ibid.,* p. 56.

6. U.T. Place, "Is Consciousness a Brain Process?" *The British Journal of Psychology,* XLVII (1956); reprinted in Borst, *ibid.,* pp. 47f.

7. U.T. Place, "Materialism as a Scientific Hypothesis," *The Philosophical Review,* LXIX (1960); reprinted in Borst, *ibid.,* p. 84.

8. B.A.O. Williams, "Personal Identity and Individuation," *Proceedings of the Aristotelean Society,* LVII (1956-57), 229.

9. Terence Penelhum, *Survival and Disembodied Existence* (London: Routledge & Kegan Paul, 1970), p. 56.

10. That it is dependent upon *present* bodily existence is more disputable. That I now have a true memory claim is not dependent upon someone else being able to check whether I use "remember" properly or consistently,

unless one contends that I cannot know for myself when I am correctly using such. Fortunately we can avoid this problem by granting the above claim, since we are not arguing for disembodied, but rather embodied, future existence.

11. Williams, *op. cit.*, p. 242.

12. *Ibid.*, p. 238.

13. *Ibid.*, p. 239.

14. C.B. Martin, *Religious Belief* (Ithaca, N.Y.: Cornell University Press, 1959), pp. 106-107.

15. It should be noted that this same reasoning can be applied to show that personal immortality is possible where man is conceived dualistically as having, rather than as being, a soul — i.e., where the soul is not held to be the locus of personal identity and the body is a necessary condition for both personal identity and the existence of the person.

CHAPTER SIX

Critique of Monism

OUR EXPOSITION OF THE DUALISTIC VIEW OF MAN WAS AC-
companied by a critique of that position. Monism likewise faces some
severe difficulties. In this chapter I intend to point out two of the
more serious objections to the Identity Theory in particular, and then
develop a broader consideration against the monistic view of man in
general.

The Problem of Identity

In defending the thesis that consciousness is a brain process, the
Identity Theorist stresses that the copula "is" is being used here, not
in the sense of predication, as in "My house is yellow," but in the
sense of identity, as in "Seven plus five is twelve." However, the
identity is not a linguistic one, which claims that statements about
mental states are reducible to or analyzable into statements about
brain processes. They deny that what is meant by mental state terms
are physio-neural processes, that "consciousness" and "brain process"
are synonyms. Rather, we are told that the identity is an empirical or
contingent one. That is, though it is not logically necessary that
consciousness be a brain process, it is a matter ultimately subject to
empirical investigation and verification that each particular state of
consciousness is identical with a particular or group of brain processes.

The Identity Theorist is making a stronger claim than that these
two can always be correlated. Mere correlation of particular states of
consciousness with certain processes of the brain would at most show
that there is a causal relation between the two different things. He
wishes to show not that the physical is only a necessary condition for
the mental, but that it is both necessary and sufficient. Thus, he

claims that the identity is a "strict identity." To understand strict identity, it is suggested that we utilize Leibniz's principle of the identity of indiscernibles: x is identical with y if and only if every property of x is a property of y, and vice versa. Presumably the Identity Theorist has grounds on which he can establish that the relation between states of consciousness and brain processes is one of strict identity, and not merely a causal connection. What are those grounds?

One Identity Theorist responds that to establish identity, not only must there be a systematic correlation between the two sets of observations, but

> we treat the two sets of observations as observations of the same event in those cases where the technical scientific observations set in the context of the appropriate body of scientific theory provide an immediate explanation of the observations made by the man in the street. Thus we conclude that lightning is nothing more than a motion of electric charges, because we know that a motion of electric charges through the atmosphere, such as occurs when lightning is reported, gives rise to the type of visual stimulation which would lead an observer to report a flash of lightning.[1]

But this condition fails to establish identity rather than causation. For any event it might be possible to have two appropriate bodies of scientific theory which would explain the observations. The one would explain the very fact that such observations are made by specifying the "true nature" of the thing or process, such that there would be held to be an identity between the phenomena observed in one way and the phenomena observed in or inferred from another set of observations. The other, incompatible with the first, would present an explanation of the phenomena rather than specifying what the phenomena "really is," and hence provide a causal explanation of the observation. If for any given observation one can provide these two, contrary scientific theories, the mere presence of either scientific theory would not enable us to decide one way or the other as to whether there is merely a causal relation between two different things, or whether there is a relation of identity. And this is precisely the case in the dispute between the monist and the dualist.

Accordingly, Identity Theorists have added the further criterion that if two things are to be identical, "the two sets of observations must refer to the same point in space and time."[2] If this condition were met, it would seem to preclude a causal explanation, for the cause and the effect, though contemporaneous during the causal activity, cannot occupy the same place at the same time.

It is quite easy to locate brain processes, for they occur in a particular place within our body. Such occurrences are verifiable by scientific instruments. But we do not give locations to states of consciousness. We do not say that my present thought of a warm summer day is occurring within my skull, that it is to the right of my thought of a chocolate ice cream cone or behind my memory of a prior wish for central air conditioning.

> If I report having suddenly thought something, the question where in my body that thought occurred would be utterly senseless. It would be as absurd to wonder whether that thought had occurred in my foot, throat, or earlobe as it would be to wonder whether that thought might have been cubical or a micron in diameter.[3]

We do, of course, locate sensations like pain in certain parts of the body, as for example, I have a toothache in my second upper molar. But we do not locate the awareness of the pain sensation anywhere.

Of course, if we stipulated that the occurrence of a brain process was the criterion for the occurrence of the thought within our head, then we could say that thinking had a place. But then the connection between thinking and the brain process would be a logical one, not an empirical identity, and hence incapable of empirical verification. There would be a connection of meaning between the statement that a certain brain process occurred in someone's head and the statement that he was thinking a certain thought in a certain place.[4] But this connection of meaning is what the Identity Theorists deny.

To return to the argument, if it makes no sense to speak of mental states occurring at the same place as brain processes, it becomes senseless to apply one of the criteria for identity, namely, that the two events occur at the same place. But without this criterion, it cannot be determined that the relation is one of identity rather than causation, for the criteria which remain are not sufficient to establish identity. Further, "if it is senseless to apply one of the criteria for identity it is also senseless to claim that there is identity."[5] Thus, not only has the Identity Theory not yet provided the grounds for showing that the relation is one of identity rather than causation, but it appears that its very claim of identity is senseless.

Defenders of the Identity Theory have replied to this criticism in at least two different ways. First, some have attempted to rescue the theory by claiming that the inapplicability of one of the criteria for identity does not count against the Identity Theory, but rather arises from a misapplication of Leibniz's principle.

The critic argues that since the property of spatiality can be meaningfully applied on one side of the identity — to brain processes — but not on the other, the Identity Theory fails to meet Leibniz's principle of the identity of indiscernibles, and hence there can be no meaningful identity claim. But, the defender replies, is Leibniz's principle applicable to all cases? It seems not. In particular, it is inapplicable where the identity proposition fails to yield a truth value (that is, where the identity proposition is neither true nor false). And when one side of the identity is senseless, the identity proposition has no truth value.

One case of senselessness particularly concerns us here. It occurs when one or both sides of the identity contain a category mistake. This is precisely what occurs when we say that a mental state is locatable. Since mental states and spatial properties belong to different categories, it is a category mistake to apply spatial predicates to mental states. Thus, any usage of spatially qualified mental states on one side of the identity proposition will result in a senseless proposition. But as such, the inability of the Identity Theory to apply spatial predicates to mental state concepts, or better, the senselessness of such talk, does not count against the theory itself. To hold that it does presupposes that Leibniz's principle is applicable in this case. But it is not, for such a proposition, as senseless, fails to yield a truth value.

This is the case not only with spatial properties. Regarding mental states and brain processes, it would seem that the properties on the two sides of the identity are frequently in different categories. That these properties cannot appear meaningfully on both sides so as to meet Leibniz's principle does not militate against the theory. The identity seems to be a cross-category identity, and hence it is still possible that the two sides refer to the same thing, and that the Identity Theory is meaningful.[6]

Though this solution programs what might turn out to be a reasonable response to the objection that the Identity Theory is senseless, much work remains to be done if this tack is pursued. For one thing, it needs yet to be spelled out what the nature of cross-category identity is. What criteria do two things with different sets of cross-category properties have to meet in order for them to be identical? This seems to be particularly pressing, now that the above analysis makes Leibniz's principle inoperative in the case of cross-category identity. We seem to be left without a criterion for identity in such instances. For another thing, if we adopt this solution, we cannot then apply the spatial criterion to the identity of mental states and brain processes. And if we cannot apply this criterion because it involves a category mistake, we are back at our original problem, for the Identity Theorist, lacking the criterion of identity of spatial location, has not yet provided a way of showing that the relation is one of identity rather than of causation. In short, though this solution shows that the Identity Theory is not *prima facie* senseless, it has *not* shown us that it is sensible or on what grounds it could be held to be meaningful, nor has it provided reasons to opt for identity over causation.

Other Identity Theorists have replied to the prior criticism by suggesting that we can "adopt a convention (which is not a change in our present rules for the use of experience words but an addition to them) whereby it would make sense to talk of an experience in terms appropriate to physical processes."[7] We can do this, it seems, because ordinary language about mental states leaves open the question of whether they have spatial location. Thus, we can adopt this convention without contradicting our present concepts of mental states, for there is nothing in our present concepts of mental states which rules out their having a spatial location.

But is it true that the adoption of this convention would not alter the meaning of statements about mental states such as to conflict with their present meaning and usage? Two important conflicts have been noted. First, certain mental state concepts are necessarily connected with behavior. As we noted in chapter four, meaning is given to certain mental state concepts in terms of their connection with our embodied behavior in the world. Thus, to say, for example, that I know how to score tennis properly requires as a necessary condition the presence at some time of an environment of an actual or hypothetical tennis match where I would perform the actual scoring. But brain state concepts do not require any such surrounding circumstances. What is meant by electro-chemical transfers within the brain is independent of the environment of an embodied individual. Thus, if we adopt the convention of spatially locating our mental processes, it would seem that we would likewise have to adopt the conditions surrounding the use of brain process concepts. But one of these conditions is the absence of the necessary condition that it be connected with behavior. Thus, we would be forced to adopt this condition with regard to mental state concepts, which would significantly alter our original criteria for the meaningful application of certain of these terms.[8]

The second conflict involved in the adoption of such a convention concerns the matter of public versus privileged access, and leads to our second major criticism of the Identity Theory.

Public vs. Privileged Access

Statements about my mental states, such as pains, wishes, or thoughts, are about something to which only I have direct access. When I report a pain in my left hand, I am speaking about an experience which only I have. It is unsharable with and imperceptible by you because you cannot feel my pain. You might know that I have a pain in my hand by watching my facial grimaces and the manner in which I am holding my hand, and by using them as criteria for saying that I am in pain. But though you might know that I am in pain, the experience of the pain itself is private.

However, statements about physical processes, about that which is locatable in space, are about things to which many individuals can have direct access. Electro-chemical movements in my brain are perceptible to a number of individuals. These movements are not private, but public.

Since the public and the private are contradictories, that which is about something private cannot at the same time be about something public, unless it is about two different things. Consequently, introspective reports about one's own mental states cannot be about the public. But to adopt the convention of applying spatial predicates to mental states would mean that reports about them would no longer be about that which is private, but about the public. It would mean that no longer do only I have direct access to my mental states such as pain or remembering; others who observed my brain states could likewise have direct access to these states. For example, it would mean that someone else could experience my toothache in my second, upper molar. But this would be to so alter our concepts of mental states as to conflict with our present usage. Therefore, the convention suggested by the Identity Theorist cannot be adopted, and the problem of using spatiality for a criterion to distinguish between a connection of identity as over against causation remains.

Furthermore, the Identity Theorist's contention that introspective statements about mental states are topic neutral must itself be questioned. The evidence just presented suggests that they do not leave it an open question of whether they are about something mental or physical. Rather, since reports of mental states are about something private, they appear to be necessarily about something which is irreducibly psychic, just as language about the physical, which is about something public, is about that which is irreducibly physical. As such, introspective reports about mental states and brain process talk cannot be merely different ways of talking about the same thing, but must refer to two different processes.[9] Linguistic evidence, far from being neutral, supports a dualism as over against the monistic Identity Theory.

Of course, this argument is successful only to the extent that ordinary language is justified as a norm, and can be accepted as accurately reporting the true state of affairs in the world. But it is these assumptions which are questioned by the Identity Theorist. Ordinary language, they argue, already comes to us with a philosophical bias. It is an idiom which is adapted, not to the facts, but to certain *beliefs* about the facts.[10] Thus, its reporting of the facts is already biased in favor of a particular belief structure — dualism. Consequently, since it presupposes a dualistic metaphysic, it cannot be taken as a neutral standard whereby to test either the monistic or dualistic view of man.

This, then, opens the door to the possibility of creating and substituting a materialistic language for the current dualistic one. The criticism of the Identity Theory based upon ordinary language thus can be circumvented by denying that the materialist need show the consistency of his theory with ordinary language.

Human Freedom

In our opening chapter we noted that the doctrine of immortality, if coupled with judgmental actions of God, could have significant moral implications for our present life. But a very serious difficulty confronts the monist at this point: the problem of adequately accounting for moral responsibility and the notion of ought, and their necessary prerequisite, human freedom. To develop why this is problematic, I will first lay out the case for the importance of maintaining that the individual is free and then examine to what extent the monistic view fails to provide adequately for human freedom.

That we are to some extent free appears as a basic datum of our subjective experience. It seems to be the case that when the alarm clock sounded this morning, I had the free choice either to remain in bed or to arise. Though I did get up, I could have done otherwise. This is not to say that there was no reason for the particular option that I chose. I desired breakfast, knowing that lunch was still many hours away. Since I wanted it, and since I had to get out of bed to acquire it, I did so, though, of course, I could have yielded to the opposite desire to remain in bed. Further, that I chose freely does not mean that there were no conditions affecting my decision. In this case, certain physiological conditions (the feeling of hunger) and certain environmental conditions (that I was in bed, the inaccessibility of food there) were factors that *in part* determined my decision. But my own experience seems to indicate that, in this case, it was *my* decision, that *I* took account of these and other factors, and though I could have done otherwise, I *freely* opted for getting out of bed rather than remaining there. That is, these factors were not sufficient conditions for the action of getting out of bed.

Moral Oughts and Moral Accountability

Though freedom itself is an important aspect of our daily life, it is ultimately significant because of its necessary connection with morality and ethics. Ethics as a branch of philosophy seeks to provide a rational basis for making sound judgments about issues which involve the moral notions of right and wrong, good and bad. In so doing, various ethical systems present principles for determining which actions are morally right and which are wrong, which ought to be morally approved and which disapproved. Thus, a particular theory will claim that one *ought* to do such and such because it is consonant with the proposed ethical principle, and *ought not* to do another act because it conflicts with the principle or a derivative thereof.

The notion of ought entails that there is more than one live option open to the individual. If I *ought* to choose to do action x, then I must be able to choose to do either action x or action y. If I cannot choose to do other than x, it is meaningless to say that I *ought* to do x; commands to do what I cannot but do are senseless. The ought simply becomes an is. Thus, freedom is entailed by the moral ought. Without freedom there is no moral ought, only an is; and without oughts, there is no morality.

Furthermore, since it is I who decide between the courses of action, I can be held morally responsible or accountable for the decision which I make. If it is a right decision, consonant with an adequate ethical principle, I am to be praised; if a wrong decision, I am blameworthy and correction is in order.

Moral accountability requires at least four things. First, the individual must have more than one option to choose from. Where there is only one course of action open, he cannot be held morally accountable for choosing and following that course. If one believes that man is free, it is difficult to present an instance where there would not be any other options to choose from, but suppose the following. Two of us are canoeing down a river and are swept by the current into some rocks. The canoe is swamped and overturned, and my partner injured. Suppose also that I had paddled and steered as best I could, but the current was so swift that it was to no avail. In this case one could not hold me morally accountable for the accident, for I had only one option — to steer to the best of my ability, but that was not sufficient to avoid the rocks.

Secondly, those options must be "live" or genuine options. There must be a reasonableness about both options, such that both are truly ones that he could reasonably choose. This involves, among other things, the possibility of a qualitative and quantitative measurability between them. It is very difficult to spell out this criterion more precisely, since it is extremely situation-relative. Perhaps an example will serve to clarify what I mean by "live." Suppose someone, holding a gun to my head and all the time threatening to pull the trigger, orders me to empty the drawer of the cash register. I do have another option besides obeying his command; I could refuse to take out the money. But it is not a reasonable or live option for me in this situation: refusal to act upon his wishes, and the possibility of my subsequent death, is not a justifiable alternative, for there exists a significant, qualitative imbalance between the options. My life is not qualitatively on a par with a limited amount of money. However, if the circumstances were altered, such that the thief orders me not to steal but to kill two other individuals, the choice between my death and the deaths of the others might indeed constitute a live option, for there now exists a measure of qualitative and quantitative comparison between my own life and that of the others.

Thirdly, one must be *aware* of the live options. To be morally accountable, one must have knowledge of the alternative courses of action and that they are live and within his ability to perform. Suppose in the canoeing incident above there was another channel around the rapids. Here, of course, I would have had another option, such that I could have steered another route and avoided the accident. But if I did not know of this channel or if I thought (mistakenly) that it was impassible, I could not be held morally accountable. Similarly with the example of the robbery; if the gun was not loaded, my refusal to take the money would not have led to my death. But though refusing to steal would then be a live option, I could not be held morally accountable for the theft because I did not know that the gun was not loaded and that this was a live option.

Fourthly, my choice between these live options must be a *free* choice. The situation must not be such that, though there are other courses of action, I am *compelled* to take a particular course, such that I could not have done otherwise. If I am compelled to take a certain course of action, moral responsibility cannot be assigned.

This is, by no means, a complete analysis of moral accountability, but I believe that it is sufficient to indicate the importance and necessity of human freedom for moral accountability and consequently moral action. Unless man is free to knowledgeably choose between live courses of action, unless he could have done otherwise, he cannot be held morally accountable for that act.

In short, we have tried to show that human freedom is entailed both by the notion of moral responsibility and by moral oughts. If I am to be held accountable for my actions, I must have been able to have done otherwise. And if I truly ought or ought not to choose a certain course of action, I must be able to choose to do other than that action. If I cannot choose to do otherwise, there is no ought, only an is. Without freedom, moral responsibility, moral oughts, and ultimately morality itself would have to be abandoned.

Monism and Freedom

It is precisely at this point that monism encounters difficulty. For the monist all of man's acts of choosing can be explained in two different language systems. Using psychological language, we say that an individual makes a decision based upon his character, attitudes, dispositions, past choices, values, and facts governing the case. He considers the alternative courses of action in terms of the desirability of the ends and consequences or according to abstract duties, and then chooses to act in a certain way. On the other hand, described physiologically, the event of choosing and then acting on that choice is a physical event which like all other events follows a cause and effect pattern. The causal conditions here are various: sensory stimuli received from the external world, energy from certain brain cells responsible for memory, electro-chemical input from other parts of the organism. These causal conditions are necessary and sufficient to bring about a particular effect — namely, the physical organism acting in a particular manner. But the psychological language of choice does not describe an event other than the physiological event which is occurring in the brain and associated regions of the body. And since that physiological event is a physical event, it must be explainable in terms of physical causes. Further, there are causal laws which connect the physical conditions of this particular choice with logically antecedent conditions, such that given these antecedent conditions, the particular choice follows. The antecedent conditions, as physical, determine the human action, such that if an individual could know what the status of those conditions was, he could predict the particular choice that would be made.

But this is to make man's choices and actions causally dependent upon prior physical conditions, which in turn find their place in the deterministic causal chain. These physical conditions — both biological and environmental — causally determine the choice such that the individual could not have chosen or acted otherwise than he did. The physical causal conditions being such and such, a certain effect necessarily follows. Thus, a freely chosen action becomes impossible; all choice and action depend upon prior physical conditions, and follow *necessarily* from them. But without freedom, man cannot be held morally accountable for his deeds, neither can there be a true ought. Thus, it would seem that an unfortunate consequence of the monistic view of man is the denial or at least seeming impossibility of human freedom and consequently of moral responsibility and morality itself.

Some monists reply that human freedom is compatible with physiological determinism. This view of freedom is often termed the Compatibility Thesis. According to this view, it is meaningful to say that, though a precise analysis of all the antecedent conditions and all other physical properties of the things connected with the event in question would have enabled us to predict what occurred, the individual is still free in that he could have done otherwise than he in fact did. By "could have done otherwise" the Compatibilist means that if certain other conditions had been fulfilled or present, an effect different in fact from what did occur would have occurred. If I had tried harder or chosen a different topic or the day had been cooler, I would have completed this chapter rather than have taken a nap. Thus, choosing not to complete this chapter today is a free act, though precise prediction of it by someone aware of all the environmental and physiological conditions present was theoretically possible. Thus, freedom must be interpreted in the hypothetical sense of ability to have done otherwise *if* the conditions had been different.

By showing in this fashion that the determinist can meaningfully predicate freedom of man, the Compatibilist has paved the way for re-introducing moral responsibility or accountability. What is it, he asks, to ascribe moral responsibility to someone for a moral action? Is it not to say that that individual's behavior can be changed by the implementation of such things as rewards and punishment? "A wrongdoer is morally responsible if and only if punishment would have affected his choice to do something wrong in the past or will now influence him to avoid such actions in the future."[11] For example, the lazy and apathetic student is morally responsible for his poor performance, and the instructor can hold him morally accountable and subject to punishment because he can do better. He could apply himself conscientiously to his next assignment, do the appropriate research, and turn in a paper of high quality. Accordingly, the instructor will punish or correct him, and consequently introduce additional causal factors in order to bring about this desired change in the student. On the other hand, a slow student cannot be held morally accountable for his poor work, for no amount of chiding or punishment will banish his slowness; his mental deficiency is the result of his genetic composition. Thus, only of the first student is it meaningful to say that he was free and could have done otherwise than he did, and that he can be held morally accountable for his poor academic performance. In this manner, then, freedom and moral responsibility are purported to be compatible with determinism and monism.[12]

But it seems odd indeed to speak of freedom, as the Compatibilist does, as the ability to have done otherwise *if* the conditions had been different. Free choice with respect to a particular event appears to refer to the possibility of there having occurred a different outcome, given the same physical state of affairs, not to the possibility of there having obtained a different set of initial conditions. Freedom operates within a certain set of given conditions; it is not a relation between different sets of conditions and their effects.

Further, this view of freedom has the unusual consequence that it reverses the positions of determinism and freedom. On this view, I am free if and only if under other circumstances I would do otherwise than I did. It stands to follow that I must be not-free if and only if under other circumstances I would not do otherwise than I now did. Now on the physicalist schema, which is a causally deterministic schema, a given cause produces a particular effect. We might say that a cause is effect-specific. But what is deterministic on the physicalist's schema is called by the Compatibilist "freedom," namely a different cause produces a different effect. Similarly, non-determinism on a physicalist schema occurs when the cause is not effect-specific, that is, when different causes can result in the same effect. But this position is called by the Compatibilist, "determinism." Thus, in effect, the Compatibilist, who is himself a physicalist, has managed to stand freedom and determinism on their heads; what is freedom is determinism, and vice versa. The self-contradictory nature of this conclusion is an unusual consequence indeed.

In conclusion, if we are to hold that man is governed by moral oughts, and that human performance or failure of performance of these yields moral responsibility, it would seem that we must reject the monistic view of man, for on this view both of these appear to be impossible because man is not free. This, I believe, constitutes a most serious objection to this view of the nature of man.

Is Man the Phoenix?

NOTES

1. U.T. Place, "Is Consciousness a Brain Process?" *British Journal of Psychology*, XLVII (1956); reprinted in *The Mind-Brain Identity Theory*, ed. C.V. Borst (N.Y.: St. Martin's Press, 1970), p. 48.

2. U.T. Place, "Materialism as a Scientific Hypothesis," *The Philosophical Review*, LXIX (1960); reprinted in Borst, *ibid.*, p. 84.

3. Jerome Shaffer, "Recent Work on the Mind-Body Problem," *American Philosophical Quarterly*, II, 2 (1965), 97.

4. Norman Malcolm, *Problems of Mind* (N.Y.: Harper & Row, 1971), p. 67.

5. Jerome Shaffer, "Could Mental States Be Brain Processes?" *Journal of Philosophy*, LVIII (1961); reprinted in Borst, *op. cit.*, p. 116.

6. James Cornman, "The Identity of Mind and Body," *Journal of Philosophy*, LIX (1962); reprinted in Borst, *ibid.*, pp. 128-129.

7. J.J.C. Smart, "Sensations and Brain Processes," *The Philosophical Review*, LXVIII (1959); reprinted in Borst, *ibid.*, p. 62.

8. Robert Coburn, "Shaffer on the Identity of Mental States and Brain Processes," *Journal of Philosophy*, LX (1963); reprinted in Borst, *ibid.*, pp. 132-133.

9. Kurt Baier, "Smart on Sensations," *Australasian Journal of Philosophy*, XL (1962); reprinted in Borst, *ibid.*, p. 105.

10. Paul Feyerabend, "Materialism and the Mind-Body Problem," *Review of Metaphysics*, XVII (1963); reprinted in Borst, *ibid.*, p. 145.

11. Gerald Dworkin, *Determinism, Free Will, and Moral Responsibility* (Englewood Cliffs, N.J.: Prentice-Hall, 1970), p. 8.

12. J.J.C. Smart, "Free Will, Praise and Blame," *Mind*, LXX (July, 1961), 291-306.

CHAPTER SEVEN

Arguments for Human Immortality

OUR ATTENTION HAS BEEN DIRECTED SO FAR TO THE FIRST question posed in chapter one: "What must man be like in order for there to be the possibility that he could live subsequent to his death?" Unfortunately, our presentation has not enabled us to opt decisively for one view of man over another; both views considered encounter difficulties. However, this inability is not detrimental to our attempt to respond to our question, for no matter which view of the nature of man one ultimately adopts, man can be immortal.

But to establish that man can be immortal does not demonstrate that he actually is immortal. Neither view of man guarantees life after death. To see whether man really will live subsequent to his death, we must turn our attention to the second question posed, "What good reasons can be given for maintaining a belief in life after death?" In this chapter I intend to present and evaluate several important arguments which purport to be good reasons. The arguments will proceed from the nature of the soul, the appeal to final causes, and the moral law.

Argument from the Nature of the Soul

The first argument which we will consider comes down to us from Plato. It is representative of those arguments which attempt to prove the immortality of the soul from the very nature of the soul. Such an argument obviously presupposes the existence of a soul, and consequently the dualistic view of man. As such, this sort of argument will have somewhat limited appeal. However, the significance of dualism is reason enough for it to warrant our close attention.

Plato contends that there is a cause of a thing being what it is or having a certain property.[1] This cause is not a material or mechanical cause but a Form or Idea.[2] Something is hot because it participates in the Form of hotness; another is cold because of the Form of coldness. Similarly with all the qualities of a thing. What makes a body healthy is the Form of health; waterfalls are beautiful because of the presence of or association with the Form of absolute beauty; a figure is square because it participates in the Form of squareness.

Plato is unfortunately (and perhaps purposefully) vague about the nature of the "causal" relation between Forms and the qualities which are called by the same name. Subsequent interpreters have differed widely on what Plato means by $αἰτία$ or cause. Some have suggested that when he speaks, for example, of the Form of beauty causing a particular thing to be beautiful, he means "cause" in the sense of efficient causation.[3] Others have argued that Plato uses $αἰτία$ in a much broader sense to mean that the relation is a logical one, such that the thing is beautiful because it possesses the characteristics which are logically necessary for something to be beautiful.[4] Both views encounter difficulties. The former runs into trouble in accounting for why the particular Form causes some things and not others to have this property, that is, in accounting for the apparent causal selectivity of a non-conscious Form; and in accounting for why a given Form has any affect on the particular object at all, since all the other Forms are acting simultaneously with equal force.[5] The latter in the apparent conflict of this interpretation with Plato's denial that what makes something beautiful is its possession of certain qualities or characteristics,[6] and its difficulty of explaining why there would have to be ontological entities (Forms) existing independently of that which possesses these characteristics or conditions. Perhaps the best we can say is, with Plato, that we cannot insist upon the precise details of the nature of this relation.

Returning to our argument, Plato argues that each of these Forms has an opposite (Hotness and Coldness; Health and Sickness; Beauty and Ugliness). A Form cannot change into or be its opposite. Hotness cannot be Coldness nor Health Sickness. Each Form is what it is.

As it is with the Forms, so it is with the particular qualities which are named after these Forms. The quality of shortness in a person cannot itself become tallness, nor heat cold. At the approach of the opposite property (when a hot thing is becoming cold or a short thing tall), either the property gives way or withdraws (as with heat) or else the property has already ceased to exist by the time the object takes on the opposite property (as with shortness).

Moreover, Plato continues, certain things[7] possess certain qualities essentially. That is, there are certain properties without which a thing cannot be the thing that it is. He presents the examples of snow and fire. Coldness belongs to snow essentially; it cannot be snow without being cold. Similarly with fire: heat is essential to fire; without heat, there can be no fire. In contrast, a certain color is not essential to being a rose; it can be red, white, yellow, or multi-colored and still be a rose.

From this Plato concludes that since Forms cannot be their opposites, and since things and properties are what they are because of their Forms, that is, because they participate in the Form of the same name, a thing which possesses a certain property essentially cannot admit of a property opposite of that which it possesses essentially. At its approach the thing itself either withdraws or ceases to exist. For example, when heat, which is the property opposite to the essential property coldness of snow, is applied to snow, the snow melts and disappears. When cold, which is the property opposite to the essential property heat of fire, is applied to fire (when the elements burning become cold), the fire is put out. Thus, the principle which Plato saw applying to the Forms themselves and the qualities called after them, he sees applying to the things which possess properties essentially — they cannot admit of properties which are opposite to their essential properties without withdrawing or ceasing to exist.

We may now take this principle and apply it to the soul and human immortality. As we noted in chapter three, since the soul is defined as the principle of life, life is an essential property of the soul. The opposite of life is death. Therefore, the soul cannot admit of death, without withdrawing or ceasing to exist. Plato thus concludes that the soul is immortal. There can be no such thing as a dead soul.

This still leaves undecided the issue whether the soul simply withdraws at death, or whether it is annihilated. Plato goes on to argue that whatever is immortal is imperishable, and whatever is imperishable cannot cease to exist. Therefore, the soul as imperishable is not annihilated at the approach of death, but rather retires from the body.

Plato's argument might be formalized as follows:

1. Forms cannot be their opposites.
2. Properties which are named after these forms cannot admit of their opposites without withdrawing or ceasing to exist.
3. A thing which has a certain property essentially cannot admit of the opposite of that property, without withdrawing or ceasing to exist.
4. The essential property of the soul is life.
5. The opposite of life is death.
6. ∴. The soul cannot admit of death without withdrawing or ceasing to exist.
7. Whatever cannot admit of death is immortal.
8. ∴. The soul is immortal.
9. Whatever is immortal is imperishable.
10. Whatever is imperishable cannot cease to exist.
11. ∴. The soul cannot cease to exist, but withdraws from that which admits of death, the body.

From what we have said in chapter three, conclusion 8 appears to be a true statement. Thus, though we may wish to question assumptions 1, 2, and 3 or the way Plato goes about showing 8 to be true, the fact that 8 appears to be true would not make this move advantageous. Since 11 appears to follow from 8-10, this leaves premises 9 and 10 which might be challenged. These premises relate to the alternatives posed in 6, that is, to the alternative of leaving or abandoning that which admits of the opposite property (while continuing itself to exist), or else of being annihilated. Plato argues that the latter is impossible for the soul, for that which is immortal is imperishable. But why is it imperishable? The answer to this is put in the mouth of Cebes, with whom Socrates is in dialog. "If what is immortal and eternal cannot avoid destruction, it is hard to see how anything else can." The introduction of the term "eternal" is unwarranted and begs the question; it has not yet been established that the soul is eternal. So let us take merely the term "immortal," and ask whether it by itself can yield Plato's desired conclusion.

Plato supports premise 9 by arguing that whatever is immortal is indestructible, and whatever is indestructible is imperishable. What does Plato mean in this passage by "destruction"? On the one hand,

Plato could mean the kind of destruction that is involved in death, that is, destruction in the sense of the termination of the life functions and organic disintegration. Interpreted in this fashion, premise 9 appears to be true. If something is immortal, it cannot die; it is not subject to the ordinary processes of organic death and decay. Moreover, this interpretation would be consonant with the principles which Plato develops in this passage. He argues that a thing cannot admit of the opposite (o) of a property (p) which comes along with or is entailed by an essential property (e). In this case, that which was immortal would not admit of destruction by the termination of the life functions (o) because o is the opposite of the property indestructibility (undying) (p) which is entailed by the essential property of being alive (e). However, if "indestructible" and consequently "imperishable" are understood in this sense, there is no reason to believe that premise 10 is true, for things can cease to exist in ways other than by organic death. They can cease to exist by physical disintegration (not linked to organic decay) or by annihilation.

If, on the other hand, Plato understands "destruction" in the broader sense of annihilation, premise 10 is true. But what about 9? If we fit "annihilation" into Plato's formula, it would then read, "The immortal soul would not admit of annihilation (o) because annihilation is the opposite of the property non-annihilability (p) which is entailed by the essential property of being alive (e)." But is p entailed by e? Does being annihilated involve for something that is alive that it should die? To assume that such is the case would beg the very question at issue, for Plato would be using this entailment to support what he is trying to prove, namely that very entailment. Consequently, the fact that something is immortal does not necessarily entail that this thing cannot cease to exist. Plato's argument appears to collapse at premises 9 and 10.

In another passage[8] Plato does present an argument to support his contention that soul is imperishable. That which comes to be must come from a first principle, but this first principle cannot come from anything else; otherwise it would not be a first principle. That which moves itself is the first principle of motion for everything else. Therefore, that which moves itself cannot come into being. Neither can it pass out of existence, for if it ceased to exist, it could not come back into existence. In such a state, the universe would become immobile, with no alternative source of motion to reintroduce motion back into it. Therefore, that which moves itself cannot begin or cease to be; it must always be in motion. The essence of soul is to move itself, for it is the principle of life and motion. Thus, soul cannot come into existence or cease to exist; it must always be in motion. Whatever is always in motion is immortal. Therefore, all soul is immortal.

It is interesting to note that in this argument Plato makes immortality a consequence of imperishability, and not vice versa, as in the argument presented in the *Phaedo*. But leaving this point aside, Plato's argument is itself critically ambiguous, for from the very outset of this passage, it is unclear whether Plato is speaking about the individual soul (every soul) or about Soul as a Form (all soul). If the latter is the proper subject of this passage, Plato has presented an argument to show that the Form of life or the First Principle or the First Mover cannot be destroyed for the reasons given, and hence is immortal. In this he anticipates later proofs for the existence of the Unmoved Mover or of God. But though for the sake of argument one might grant him his proof that the Form Soul or First Principle cannot be annihilated, this does not entail that individual souls cannot be so affected. The individual soul is the principle of life for a particular being, but it is not a Form. Neither is it a First Mover in the sense of being the source of all motion. Hence, proving the immortality of Soul as a First Principle does not aid us in showing that the individual soul is immortal. If the former is the proper subject of this passage, that is, if the argument is concerned with individual souls, then the argument is not sound, for the drastic consequences of universal immobility which he foresees were the self-mover to be destroyed need not follow upon the destruction of the individual soul. So long as there were in continued existence some First Mover or First Principle of motion, there would continue to be a source of motion in the universe. Likewise, there seems to be no good reason why individual souls might not be generated from some Eternal Soul. But being so generated would mean that they were not eternal. Thus, no matter which way one understands Plato, the argument fails to provide argumentative support for the crucial and questioned premises in the *Phaedo* which seek to prove personal immortality.

In summary, Plato's argument for immortality of the individual soul appears to fail in that he cannot prove the point at issue, that is, that the individual soul withdraws from the body rather than is annihilated. Arguments such as the one presented in the *Phaedrus* might establish the eternality of Soul as a Form or First Principle, but not the immortality of the individual soul.

Arguments from Final Cause

A second sort of argument given to establish the reality of human immortality is teleological in nature. That is, from considerations of the end for which man was created or for which man strives one can conclude that he must be immortal. Two such arguments were developed by Thomas Aquinas.

Aquinas held that man was made for an ultimate end, which is happiness.[9] But happiness cannot be achieved either in this life or in a life where the soul lives without a body. That it cannot be achieved in this life is evident from the changeableness of an individual's fortune (sometimes things work in our favor, but other times not), the weakness of the human body (it tires easily in the pursuit of happiness and is soon dissatisfied with the level of happiness achieved), and the imperfection and instability of human knowledge and virtue (I know my world imperfectly and without certainty and am too quickly able to forget or not put into practice what I have learned).[10] Neither can happiness be achieved by a soul separated from its body, for in such a state man is incomplete. But since man cannot have been made in vain, he must be able to achieve the end for which he was made. Therefore, the soul must continue to live after this life, united with the self-same body.

We might formalize the argument as follows:

1. If man were unable to obtain the last end for which he was made, he would be made in vain.

2. Man cannot be made in vain.

3. ∴ Man is able to obtain the last end for which he was made.

4. This last end is happiness or beatitude.

5. ∴ Man is able to obtain happiness or beatitude.

6. Happiness or beatitude cannot be achieved either (a) in this life, or (b) in a life where the soul exists without its body.

7. ∴ The soul continues to live after this life, in conjunction with the self-same body that died.

Since conclusions 3, 5, and 7 appear to follow from their respective premises, let us direct our attention to Aquinas's premises, beginning first with premises 4 and 6.

Most people, I think, would agree with the contention of premise 4 that happiness is the ultimate goal of man or the final end for which he was made. Indeed, this view has formed the basis of most proposed ethical theories. To cite just one example, Aristotle contends that the good is that at which all things aim, and the chief good — that at which all things aim and which is desired for its own sake — is happiness. By happiness he does not mean a momentary feeling of pleasure or an ever-changing and completely transitory state of being. Neither is it a disposition, for then one might be happy while existing as a vegetable. Rather, "happiness is an activity of the soul in accordance with virtue . . . in a complete life."[11]

> The happy man will be happy throughout his life; for always, or by preference to everything else, he will be engaged in virtuous action and contemplation, and he will bear the chances of life most nobly and altogether decorously, if he is "truly good" and "foursquare beyond reproach."[12]

Though events both good and bad will befall the good and happy man, he will not vacillate with every change of fortune; "he will not be moved from his happy state easily or by any ordinary misadventures." He will, like a military general, persevere in the face of adversity by continuing to perform virtuous actions; therein lies his happiness.

However, if "happiness" is understood in this sense, then the truth of premise 6 appears doubtful. The kind of happiness spoken of above seems attainable in this present existence, despite what Aquinas calls the changeableness of human fortune, the weakness of the body, and the imperfection and instability of human knowledge and virtue. For example, Aristotle suggests that man can attain complete happiness in this life if he engages in the activity of reason or contemplation throughout his life. Contemplation will bring the greatest and most perfect happiness, for happiness extends as far as the life of reason does. But since we are physical creatures as well as intellectual souls, it need be accompanied by other kinds of virtue and some external prosperity,

> for our nature is not self-sufficient for the purpose of contemplation, but our body also must be healthy and must have food and other attention.

Still, we must not think that the man who is to be happy cannot be supremely happy without external goods; for self-sufficiency and action do not involve excess, and we can do noble acts without ruling earth and sea. . . . Solon, too, was perhaps sketching well the happy man when he described him as moderately furnished with externals but as having done the noblest acts, and lived temperately.[13]

Happiness as here described is within the grasp of mortal man. Rhetorically Aristotle asks, "Why then should we not say that he is happy who is active in accordance with complete virtue and is sufficiently equipped with external goods, not for some chance period but throughout a complete life?"[14]

Returning to Aquinas's argument, if premise 6 is to be true, he must understand "happiness" in a way quite different from Aristotle. And in fact this is precisely the case. Aquinas argues that man's ultimate happiness is to be found in man's most excellent and unique operation, directed toward the most perfect objects and necessary things.[15] Accordingly, it cannot be found in such things as pleasures of the body (eating, drinking, and sex), for these are not ultimate ends, but seek something beyond themselves, namely preservation of the body and procreation of children. It does not reside in honor or glory, for these are not the end of man's own action (not done or performed by him) but are bestowed on him. Neither does it consist of goods, either external wealth, which is not an end in itself since it is sought in order to acquire other things, or internal goods such as health, beauty, or strength, for these are imperfect and easily lost. Neither is man's ultimate happiness to be found in moral activities, for that which is ultimate cannot be directed toward further ends. But moral virtues seek further ends — bravery is directed toward victory and peace, justice toward peace between men.

Man's ultimate end or happiness is to be found in that which is supremely the end of all. God is the supreme good, and consequently the supreme end of all. Therefore, man's ultimate happiness is to be found in the knowledge and possession of God. But we cannot know or possess God perfectly in this life. Our present knowledge of God by natural reason or demonstration can be erroneous and uncertain; our knowledge of God by faith is an act of the will, not of the intellect. In faith the intellect is imperfect because it does not grasp the object of its assent. Thus, if knowledge of God were to consist in this, man's potentialities would not be perfected. The knowledge of God which is man's ultimate happiness is the immediate knowledge of him, the supernatural vision of God. But this is not attainable in this life (except in rare moments of rapture); hence there must be an afterlife in which man is perfected in the immediate apprehension of God.[16]

But why must the ultimate end consist of that which is perfect? Why cannot the limited be ultimate? Aquinas's response is that, by its very nature, the ultimate end is that beyond which the agent seeks nothing further. Since the imperfect can have something beyond it which could be the object of desire, namely the perfect, and since there cannot be an infinity of ends, the imperfect cannot be the ultimate.[17] Hence, the ultimate end must be found in the perfect. For man, this is the perfection of his potentialities through his most perfect operation, namely, the knowledge and possession of that which is itself perfect, which is God.

But though this argument shows that the ultimate end, if such there be, must be found in and directed toward the perfect, it remains to be shown that man has an ultimate end so interpreted. That is, this argument demonstrates the truth of premise 6; but what about premise 4? Aquinas argues for the truth of 4 as follows:

8. The movement of every agent tends to something definite.

9. Tending to something definite is to act for an end.

10. ∴ Every agent tends to or acts for an end.

11. An end must be fitting or appropriate to the agent (otherwise it would not act to attain it).

12. That which is fitting for something is good for it.

13. ∴ Every agent tends to something good for it.

14. ∴ Good as such is the end of every agent's actions.

15. ∴ That which is supremely good is the supreme end of every agent's actions.

16. God is the supreme good.

17. ∴ God is the supreme or ultimate end of every agent's actions.

18. The ultimate end is called happiness or beatitude.

19. ∴ God is man's ultimate happiness or beatitude.[18]

There are two moves in this argument which merit closer inspection. The first is from 13 to 14. In 13, that which is the end of an agent's action is something which is good for it. Here "good" refers to a particular thing which is person-relative: it is something beneficial or good *for* the agent. But in 14, it is no longer a particular thing which is the end, but an abstract *good;* it is no longer a good which is person-relative, but the *universal* good. But does 14 follow from 13? For it to follow, the assumed major premise — to tend for something which is good for a thing is to tend for the good *per se* — must be true. That it is not conceptually or necessarily true follows from the fact that it is perfectly conceivable and not self-contradictory to say that someone could pursue what is beneficial for himself without pursuing the good *per se,* or that what is beneficial for himself is not consonant with the good. That it is not empirically true follows from those cases of individuals known to each of us who do not care what the good is or even believe that there is such, so long as they can do what is best for themselves. They do not act for any universal good or for that which would be profitable to others; neither will they sacrifice what they think is personally beneficial even if shown it is not consonant with the good. In such a case, the end for which they act would be different from the good *per se.* Aquinas can show this assumed premise to be true only by appealing to the dubious metaphysical doctrine of participation, which contends that each particular good participates in the one good. Accordingly, if one rejects this questionable philosophical doctrine, the truth of 14 does not follow from 13 and the assumed major premise.

Secondly, suppose that we grant 14 for the sake of the argument; does 15 follow from 14? There seems to be nothing about the concepts of the good *per se* or acting to achieve it which would entail that whatever acts for the good *per se* acts for or tends toward a supreme end or Good. Indeed, agents might limit their actions to finite, intermediate ends or goods, without ever seeking to attain the ultimate of perfection. In fact, considering the nature of the agents, that they are finite, imperfect, and limited in power and knowledge, it would seem most reasonable to expect that they would act for or tend to finite ends. Even the happiness intended, as Aristotle points out, is directly relative to the nature of the being who seeks it. That is, the agent seeks a happiness which is fitting to its nature, which, if imperfect, would be an imperfect happiness.

Aquinas responds that "all action and movement is for some perfection."[19] But this is merely asserted, and not argued for. Indeed, to assume it is to beg the question, for this is the very point at issue. Hence, conclusion 15, which is an existential statement about man's actions and their end, has not been proven true. The consequence of this is that his argument fails to show that in reality man has an ultimate end such as perfection.

In short, Aquinas is faced with a dilemma. If man has an ultimate end, which is happiness as understood in the sense described by Aristotle, then premise 4 appears to be true, but premise 6 false. If, on the other hand, we follow Aquinas in interpreting happiness as a perfection, that is, as the perfect attainment of that which is perfect (God), then premise 6 is apparently true, but Aquinas has not proven that man has an ultimate end so interpreted. At least the argument by which he attempts to prove this is not sound. Indeed, given man's finitude and imperfections, it seems that premise 4, so understood, is false. And if either premise 4 or premise 6 is false, we no longer have a sound proof of human immortality.

Objection can likewise be raised against premise 1, where Aquinas contends that man would be made in vain if he could not achieve his ultimate end. Would God's creation be compromised if man failed to achieve his ultimate end, no matter what other ends he did realize? I see no reason to think that this would be the case. For instance, if man achieved limited fulfillment of human potential or partially realized a life of happiness, perhaps in the manner suggested by Aristotle, or if this man came to know God in his own limited way, actualized his intellectual capacity through contemplation of what truth could be known given human limitations, and lived a virtuous life, there would seem to be no grounds for the negative valuation — "made in vain" — to be stamped across his ledger. Aquinas apparently is assuming that anything short of achievement of perfection is sufficient grounds for such a negative valuation. But I fail to see why this is the case. Hence, the implication in premise 1 can be denied, with the consequence that Aquinas's proof of immortality fails.

Argument from Natural Desires

A second argument developed by Aquinas proceeds from the natural desire of man. All conscious beings, he argues, desire to exist. Animals manifest this desire on the sensory level; witness their flight from danger and their struggle to survive. But the senses can know existence only here and now, only in the present. Man, however, is unique in that he desires to exist, not merely here and now, but forever. This desire for future existence is possible because man by his intellect can conceptually understand what existence and future time are. A natural desire cannot be in vain. Therefore, man is immortal. [20]

This argument, too, is fraught with problems. First, is it true that man has a natural desire for immortality? How can we ascertain that eternal life is a *natural* human desire, and not a learned one? Not everyone desires to be immortal; many with whom I am acquainted consider such a prospect to be evil indeed. Neither can one discern from human actions whether it is natural or not. The drive for immediate self-preservation, Aquinas argues, should not be confused with the drive for immortality. If it is, the argument proves too much, in that it proves that all living things strive for and hence will be granted immortality.

Secondly, are there adequate grounds for making this essential distinction between the animal drive for self-preservation and the human desire for immortality? The basis of Aquinas's distinction is the animal's inability and man's ability to conceive of existence beyond the here and now, for all time. But though there is a qualitative difference in the epistemic aspect — that is, between the animal's *perception* of existence here and now and the human *conception* of eternal existence, in that the one is a percept and the other a concept — the difference between the kinds of existence desired is only quantitative. The animal strives for continued existence at this (and every) moment in time; man desires continued existence for an indefinite future at this (and every) moment in time. If we take each of the momentary desires for continued existence on the part of the animal, and put them in a continuous series, we get an unending series of momentary, natural desires for existence. Applying the principle that natural desires cannot be in vain to this, we get what amounts to animal immortality. The animal, desiring to exist at each moment, would continue to exist at each moment, and hence would exist indefinitely. It might not have a specific desire for immortality *per se*, nor can it conceive of its desire in these terms. But since at each moment it has a natural desire to continue to exist, it would seem that it too, by this same principle, would be immortal. Thus, Aquinas's distinction is important for deciding what the animal does and does not know, but in distinguishing the temporal consequence of the animal's desires from those of man, it is not a significant difference at all. Both would yield the same result of unending existence, which for Aquinas proves too much.

Finally, can the principle that a natural desire cannot be in vain be supported? The evidence of nature is quite to the contrary, for many natural desires are in vain. Even the momentary desires for continued existence on the part of animals are continually and viciously being thwarted. The principle invoked here seems more dubious than the conclusion of human immortality deduced from it.

Argument from the Moral Law

A third kind of proof for human immortality commences from moral premises. In general, the moral argument asserts that since finite human existence is insufficient either to achieve the moral ideal or to provide an adequate basis on which to recommend the performance of good rather than evil, man must be immortal.

The former thesis was developed by the German philosopher Immanuel Kant. Kant contends that if our will is to be directed by the moral law, it must take as its object the achievement of the highest good.[21] That is, we are commanded by the moral law to attain the highest good.

Morever, if we are to make the highest good our object, we must be able to achieve it. If it were unachievable, we could not reasonably be commanded to attain it. We cannot be bound to, nor commanded to order our lives according to the universal dictates of, a moral law which demands the impossible. Therefore, if we are to live under the moral law, we must be able to achieve the highest good. We may liken it to running a race. If we know at the outset that the goal or end-tape is unattainable, we cannot reasonably command the runner to achieve it or even to run the race at all. Ability to succeed or attain the goal is a necessary condition for reasonably commanding participation.

What is the highest good for Kant? Kant suggests that an essential or supreme condition of the highest good is virtue — the complete fitness of one's intentions or motives to the moral law. There are, he argues, universal moral laws whose denial leads to contradiction. Virtue is the alignment of our own wills with these laws, such that we act solely out of respect for these moral laws and not out of inclination

126

(for example, self-love or sympathy) or to achieve any end such as pleasure or fame. To act virtuously, then, is to act from the right motive — to do one's duty for duty's sake. The highest good would be *always* to act from the right motive, and this is holiness.

Since holiness is perfect virtue or the complete fitness of one's intentions to the moral law, and since complete fitness is the supreme condition of the highest good, and since the highest good must be attainable, holiness must be attainable. But no finite creature on earth can ever be holy. Therefore, if we are to achieve holiness, an endless progress is necessary. But endless progress is possible only under the presupposition that man has an infinitely enduring existence, that he is immortal. Consequently, since the possibility of achievement of the highest good is a prerequisite for the performance of the moral good under the moral law, and since immortality is a prerequisite for the possibility of achieving the highest good, if he is to live under the moral law, man must be immortal. That is, if we are to have an adequate ethic, if we are to be required to live under the moral law, we must at the same time postulate an infinite time for the highest good to be realized. Human immortality is a necessary postulate of a valid moral law.

We might formalize Kant's argument as follows:

1. If our will is to be directed by the moral law, it must take as its object the achievement of the highest good.

2. If we are to be required to pursue the highest good, the achievement of the highest good must be possible.

3. ∴ In order to live under the moral law, the achievement of the highest good must be possible.

4. Complete fitness of intentions or motives to the moral law is the supreme condition or part of the highest good.

5. Holiness is the complete fitness of intentions to the moral law.

6. ∴ In order to live under the moral law, holiness must be possible.

7. Holiness cannot be acquired in this world.

8. ∴ Endless progress is necessary to achieve holiness.

9. Endless progress is possible only under the presupposition of the infinitely enduring existence and personality of the individual.

10. ∴ To achieve holiness man must be immortal.

11. . . . In order to live under the moral law, man must be immortal.

The crucial, and I believe questionable, premise is the second one. Kant here is contending that the highest good must be realizable, not merely in part, but completely, for it is the "complete fitness of intentions to the moral law" which Kant deems necessary on our part to fulfill the highest good. Only a life of holiness — a perfection — will be consonant with the *summum bonum.*

But why must one be able to realize completely the highest good in order for one to pursue it? Kant's response is that it is achievable because it is commanded by the moral law. If we are to have an adequate moral law and expect it to be determinative of our behavior, it cannot command us to attain that which is unattainable. If it did, it would be directing us toward empty and imaginary ends, and would thereby be false.[22]

But is this the case? I think not. A goal does not have to be completely realizable for us to be commanded or to attempt to perform actions dictated by it. Such goals are ideals toward which a man strives. Ideals may be at best only partially realizable, but that does not destroy their capacity to function as real directives to human action. The impossibility of their complete realization makes them neither empty nor imaginary. They are not empty because they have a positive content which can direct our action; they are not imaginary because they constitute a real objective of human moral endeavor.

Above we suggested the analogy of running a race. In our era with its stress on victory, it might seem true that one would not recommend to his son that he enter a race unless he could be assured at least a chance of winning. But this is not the only condition under which participation can be recommended. One could encourage and even command competing in the race for the personal benefit which would be gained from the act of competing and from the physical exercise, even if one could never win or even complete the race. The fact that the activity could result in some personal good is sufficient to recommend it. Similarly with the moral law. That man cannot achieve perfection or holiness does not mean that he cannot acquire some lasting, personal benefit from attempts to perform according to the moral law. By the achievement of some moral good he will be better off morally than if he had not attempted to do the good at all. Even if we follow Kant's suggestion and disregard such hypothetical ends as personal benefit, we can say that one should do the good despite the impossibility of achieving holiness because of the resulting increased perfection of the rational will, or because the practical reason commands it to do such duties, or simply because such actions are the right things to do and reason recognizes that it is so. In none of these cases must the highest good be completely realizable, and yet each provides sufficient reason to make the command a reasonable one. In short, the possibility of the achievement of some good, and not necessarily the complete realization of the highest good, is sufficient to recommend or command that we live under the moral law.

Kant defends himself by suggesting that this would be to water down and weaken the moral law, and ultimately degrade it, for we have fashioned the moral law according to the weaknesses and imperfections of the human being. We have made the moral law more lenient (indulgent), so that it fits the man rather than man the moral law.

But this is not the case. We have not suggested in our criticism that the moral law itself be changed or altered to fit the weaknesses, frailties, and passions of the man. The ultimate good still is an ideal which, if not completely realizable, is partly attainable. All we have suggested is that the possibility of achievement of this ideal of perfection is not required in order to recommend that we perform according to the moral law. The content of the law remains the same. All we have denied are the conditions Kant deems necessary for obedience to its commands.

Returning to the argument for immortality, if our contention is correct, then premise 2 is false, and conclusions 3, 6, and 11 do not necessarily follow as being true. That is, if we need not have complete realization of the highest good, if only partial realization will suffice to make the command to pursue it reasonable, then immortality is not a postulate of or required by the moral law. Man, in his finite human existence, can achieve a partial realization of the highest good by performing some actions consonant with the moral law for duty's sake alone. Hence, Kant has not given us a sound proof of human immortality.

Argument from the Sanction for Doing Good

A second moral argument contends that immortality must be a reality if we are to be provided with an adequate reason for doing good rather than evil. Ethical philosophers, preachers, teachers, and parents all command or recommend that we do the good and avoid the evil. We are told not to kill, steal, cheat, lie, commit adultery, or disobey; we are instructed to be temperate, honest, loving, unselfish, and obedient. But why, one might ask, should I follow these recommendations? Why should I do good rather than evil? The answer which is frequently given is that it is in my best interests to do good and not evil. If I disregard these and other moral recommendations, I will not be able to secure what I want from life. If I do wrong, others will follow in my footsteps. If I cheat, they will have no compunction not to cheat me; if I lie, they will feel no obligation to tell me the truth; if I steal, they will take what is mine. I will not be able to succeed at business because I will constantly be defrauded; my home life will be a shambles because of dishonesty, selfishness, and lack of trust. Since this state of affairs would make life unbearable and unrewarding, I must do the good rather than the evil. A successful life requires keeping the moral law.

The objection which can be raised at this point is that the moral life frequently does not provide what one wants out of life, nor does keeping the moral law make life successful. The complaint of the Psalmist is heard repeatedly: why do evildoers prosper while the righteous suffer? He who does the right suffers anguish and grief; he is persecuted and taken advantage of by the crafty man of no principle.[23] Moreover, one can imagine — if one is not already personally acquainted with such individuals — a person who has led a successful life characterized by injustice and wrongdoing. He has succeeded in that he has obtained what he wanted out of life; his life as he planned it has been complete and happy. Glaucon's story of Gyges and the magic ring is often used to illustrate the point. Gyges found a ring which, when its bezel was rotated in a particular manner, enabled him to become invisible. He succeeded in being sent to the royal court, where by using the powers of the ring he seduced the queen, murdered the king, and seized control of the kingdom.[24] By every standard (except the moral one) Gyges must be judged to have led a successful life: marriage to a beautiful woman, a kingly coronation, acquisition of wealth, and the establishment of a royal line.

The reply is made to this that we must not judge the success or failure of the moral life solely in terms of our present finite existence. This is to take much too limited a scope for evaluation. The life hereafter must also be considered in assessing its success or failure. In the future existence, justice, truth, honesty, and goodness will be rewarded, and evil punished.

Applying this to the problem of the reality of immortality, the argument is made that an adequate ethic requires a sanction for doing good. Such a sanction is to be found in the fact that, ultimately, goodness will be rewarded and evil punished. But this presupposes that man is immortal. Therefore, immortality is a prerequisite for an adequate ethic.

If we believe that God exists, we cannot imagine that anyone who disobeys his laws and commandments will ultimately be judged to have led a good life. God must reward the good and demonstrate that evil actions do not pay. But for this to occur, for justice to be ultimately served, man must be immortal. Therefore, immortality is a prerequisite for the justification of the pursuit of the good: only if there is life after death can one justify the contention that one should do good rather than evil.

This argument, however, seems to reduce morality to a concern for advantage. That is, it appears to reduce the ought to an is. Why *ought* I to do such and such? Because it will bring me certain things or have advantageous consequences. But are the virtues of kindness, goodness, justice, and honesty justifiable only in terms of what they produce?

> When we are confronted with two men, one of whom loves justice, kindness and generosity, without thought for what they bring, while the other thinks only of what they bring, do we not want to say different things about them? Do we not want to say that only one of them loves justice while the other's love is a mere pretence, a façade? That this is so is shown by the fact that when the situation changes, when it no longer pays to be good, the man who pursued the virtues only for external reasons soon gives up his love of virtue. But, notice, even if the change in the situation never comes about, even if it always remains the case that it pays to be good, the difference between the two men remains unaltered, for what determines that difference is the relation within which they stand to the pursuit of virtue.[25]

In reducing moral considerations to considerations of advantage, we have "falsified the character of moral considerations." What is commended is no longer morality itself or the virtues themselves, but the advantage one can get from them. We are asked to do good because of what we get from it. But is it not the contention of morality that we

131

should do the good because it is good?

The connection between morality and advantage is only a contingent, not a necessary, relation. That there is a God to guarantee that the good will always result in the advantageous does not make the connection necessary. It is contingent because "it is always possible to distinguish between a concern for moral considerations and a concern for advantage."[26] We should do good and perform virtuously because it is good and virtuous. Therefore, the reality or unreality of immortality becomes irrelevant to recommending the performance of good here and now. We are to do good because it is good, not because we will be rewarded in the afterlife.

If, therefore, the appeal to advantage as a sanction for doing good is illegitimate because it eliminates the distinctively moral element, we no longer have the grounds for concluding that immortality is a prerequisite for an adequate ethic, and that man is immortal.

Conclusion

What can we conclude from the above? It appears that, at least insofar as we have considered them, the arguments which have been traditionally considered to have proven the reality of immortality are not successful. None of them, it seems, is a sound argument.

Some might object that we have misinterpreted the function of the traditional arguments, that they were meant to be pieces of persuasive reasoning, not formally deductive arguments. But if they are not sound, one wonders how they can be legitimately used as persuasive devices to support the reality of immortality. Antony Flew humorously refers to this method as the Ten Leaky Buckets Method. If each argument is unsound, by putting together ten unsound arguments we cannot establish the probability of something, though we might make it appear deceptively plausible. Flew's point is applicable here. This being the case, perhaps it is best at this juncture to suspend judgment on the issue of the reality of immortality, concluding that we possess no decisive evidence to enable us to opt for one view over another. But before we do this, let us turn our attention to a different kind of argument, one which might be termed an historical-theological argument.

NOTES

1. Plato, *Phaedo*, 100b-107a.

2. "But to call things like that causes is too absurd. If it were said that without such bones and sinews and all the rest of them I should not be able to do what I think is right, it would be true. But to say that it is because of them that I do what I am doing, and not through choice of what is best — although my actions are controlled by mind — would be a very lax and inaccurate form of expression. Fancy being unable to distinguish between the cause of a thing and the condition without which it could not be a cause!" *Ibid.*, 99a4-b4.

3. Aristotle, *On Generation and Corruption*, 335B7ff; R. Hackforth, *Plato's Phaedo* (N.Y.: The Liberal Arts Press, 1952), pp. 143-145.

4. Gregory Vlastos, "Reasons and Causes in the Phaedo," *The Philosophical Review*, LXXVIII (1969), 291-325.

5. *Ibid.*, 304-305.

6. Plato, *op. cit.*, 100c3-d6.

7. Hackforth (*op. cit.*, pp. 151-157) interprets Plato as talking about Forms and not individual things in this passage. The consequence of this is to interpret Plato's argument for immortality as proving the immortality of the Form of the soul, and not of the individual soul. His interpreted translation of ὅσα in 104b8 as "Form" is, I think, mistaken.

8. *Phaedrus*, 245c5-246a2.

9. *Summa Theologica*, Supplement to Pt. III, Q. 79, A. 2.

10. *Ibid.*, Q. 75, A. 1.

11. Aristotle, *Nicomachean Ethics*, Bk. I, ch. 7, 1098a16-18; ch. 13, 1102a5.

12. *Ibid.*, Bk. I, ch. 10, 1100b17-21.

13. *Ibid.*, Bk. X, ch. 8, 1178b34-1179a12.

14. *Ibid.*, Bk. I, ch. 10, 1101a14-16.

15. Aquinas, *Summa Contra Gentiles*, Bk. III, ch. 35.

16. *Ibid.*, ch. 17, 37-40, 60-62.

17. *Ibid.*, ch. 2.

18. *Ibid.*, ch. 2-3, 16-20, 24-25.

19. *Ibid.*, ch. 3.

20. *Summa Theologica*, Pt. I, Q. 75, A. 6.

21. *Critique of Practical Reason*, Bk. II, ch. 2, IV (122-124).

22. *Ibid.*, Bk. II, ch. 2, I (114).

23. Psalms 13:2; 22:1-21.

24. Plato, *The Republic*, Bk. II, 359c-360e.

25. D.Z. Phillips, *Death and Immortality* (N.Y.: St. Martin's Press, 1970), p. 29.

26. *Ibid.*, p. 30.

CHAPTER EIGHT

The Historical-Theological Argument

IN LIEU OF SOUND PHILOSOPHICAL PROOFS FOR LIFE AFTER death, I want to explore a different kind of argument which comes to the same conclusion. This argument, which might be termed an historical-theological argument, was initially suggested by the first-century persecutor-turned-evangelist, Paul. In his discourse on life after death,[1] St. Paul contends that if there be no resurrection from the dead, then not only has Christ himself not risen, but our faith in him is wasted effort. We remain in the sinful state from which we thought we were freed. But, he goes on to argue, the *fact* of the matter is that Christ not only died for our sins, but was given new life on the third day following his crucifixion. That the event really occurred is attested by the many witnesses to the living Lord. This event, the resurrection of Christ, is the basis of the promise of our own re-creation, for it is in and through Christ that all will be made alive at his second coming. Thus, because Jesus Christ historically died and historically lived after his death, even though we die, we shall live again. The historical fact is the ground for the theological promise.

The reason for calling this argument an historical-theological one should be evident. The historical aspect is the claim that some-one (Jesus Christ) has in fact lived subsequent to his death, and that such an astounding event is well authenticated. The theological aspect of the argument provides the interpretation and meaning of this event with respect to our own future. It claims that God has revealed to man the promise that the God who renewed the life of Jesus will, through that same individual, renew the life of each individual. The historical fact that this has already been performed for one individual in human history is both that which *makes possible* our own immortality (for it is through the living Jesus Christ that we shall be raised,

135

such that if he had not been historically raised to new life, we would have no way to attain immortality) and the *guarantee* that God's promise that we shall be re-created will be fulfilled. This is what is meant by the claim of this argument that the historical reality is the ground of the theological faith.

It should be obvious from the outset that we are faced with an entirely different sort of argument from those considered in the previous chapter. The latter were a priori arguments, which staked their validity upon the canons of logic and reason. But Paul's argument is of a different sort, for it combines the historical or a posteriori with the a priori (theological propositions about God). In commencing with an historical claim, it is arguing from experience, and in particular, from an event which is no longer directly verifiable. Thus, any evaluation of the soundness of this argument will have to utilize historical methodology and criteria as well as logical ones. Since historical criteria can yield only probability, the initial premise and hence the conclusion can be at best probable. As such the conclusion cannot possess the kind of certainty which those in the previous chapter, if they had followed validly from true premises, could have.

Secondly, this argument contains within it or presupposes a backlog of theological presuppositions. It presupposes that God exists, that he can reveal himself sufficiently to make promises, that he is trustworthy enough to keep his promises, and that he is powerful enough to be able to implement them. Though one might attempt to deduce these theological assertions from certain empirical data and conceptual truths, as, for example, Thomas Aquinas did, the historical-theological argument as first presented makes no such attempt. Paul from his Jewish tradition merely assumes this theological content. For the sake of manageability, we shall do the same, concentrating our attention on the first part of the argument (the claims of historicity) and its relation to the second part (as ground for faith or hope).

Can Faith Be Given Historical Support?

One objection which has been raised against the historical-theological argument arises from the use which the theological aspect of the argument makes of the historical. The objection is that it is a mistake to ground theological faith on the empirical, as the argument has done with history, and this for several reasons. First, such a grounding makes faith subject to empirical disproval or refutation. By casting doubt upon the truth of the essential assertions of that support, the faith itself is placed in jeopardy. By showing that the propositions are false, the ground of faith is removed and the house of faith erected thereupon collapses. If one could show that there did not exist any such individual as Jesus of Nazareth, that he was not crucified, or that his resurrection was not an historical event, and if one had inseparably linked his faith to any or all of these contentions, then the results of historical inquiry could be destructive of that faith. But this is to prostitute one's own faith — that which gives meaning to one's own individual existence — to the researches and conclusions of others. It is to make one's faith depend upon the knowledge and information compiled by the historian, who might himself not have faith. Chained to history, faith can be destroyed by the work of the unbeliever. This contradicts the true nature of faith. Faith is a personal appropriation of that which gives meaning to one's own existence. It is my response to a reality which discloses itself to me. So interpreted, faith is the result of *my* own discovery of what gives significance to my life; it is the record of *my* response to the personal initiatives of the divine. What others conclude might direct my attention to appropriate objects of faith or trust or be a witness to their own faith; their inquiries might force me to revise or refine the way I view the world or understand my faith. But they can neither create faith in me nor destroy a faith which I already possess. Faith stands apart from history.

Secondly, such a relation between faith and history eliminates the challenge of faith. Faith is a venture. It is the commitment of oneself to that which is uncertain, unproved, perhaps even paradoxical. But to ground faith on matters of empirical inquiry is to base faith on certainty, and consequently to remove the element of venture. Faith now becomes a matter of wisdom; it would be an act of foolishness to reject knowledge. The demand of risk, of really believing, is thus lost.

> If we insist that the events [surrounding the resurrection] must be viewed in "physical" terms, . . . if we insist that faith must be faith in the reliability of the witnesses and that the legitimation of Jesus must be thus secured before we can commit ourselves to him — if we say that true faith is impossible without this legitimation — then we are rejecting

faith as a challenge, as a venture. And that means that we are refusing to believe.[2]

Finally, if faith does require historical support, we are in sorry shape indeed, for as historians we cannot excavate to the historical substructure of the New Testament documents. That which really occurred is lost forever beneath the kerygma and interpretation of the early Church. All that we can know is that a Jewish prophet named Jesus

> lived and preached and interpreted the Old Testament; that he deplored Jewish legalism, abandoned ritual purifications, and breached the Sabbath commandment; that he was not an ascetic, and was a friend of harlots and sinners; that he showed sympathy to women and children, and performed exorcisms.[3]

What else is recorded about this man, including his resurrection, is the early Church's mythical reinterpretation of his life and teaching. Thus, there is insufficient knowable and reliable historical data on which to found faith.

But what does this lack of historical knowledge and support matter, the objector continues. Faith is based not on the results of historical research, but rather on preaching or kerygma. "Faith comes by hearing, and hearing by the Word of God." Through the encounter with the Word, we have the eschatological hope of immortality. God comes to each of us, discovering us in our fear of death and despair, assuring us of his providence in the world and his control of the future. History has nothing to add to or detract from this.

> Real Easter faith is faith in the word of preaching which brings illumination. If the event of Easter Day is in any sense an historical event additional to the event of the cross, it is nothing else than the rise of faith in the risen Lord, since it was this faith which led to the apostolic preaching. The resurrection itself is not an event of past history. All that historical criticism can establish is the fact that the first disciples came to believe in the resurrection.[4]

Since, therefore, the historical aspect is not of interest or significance to the Christian faith and belief, some critics insist that it is a mistake to argue as St. Paul has done. To ground a theological assertion or item of faith upon the historical is to engage once again upon mythologizing. It is to bind faith to something which can be disputed

and refuted, to that which inevitably comes couched in some transitory world view. The item of faith must stand alone, accepted in faith
and reinterpreted in light of our present existential categories and
human situation. It must be seen in its overall eschatological perspective, not in a narrow historical framework. The Easter legends of the
empty tomb and appearances are of no consequence to faith in Christ
or faith in God's eschatological designs for men.

Faith and History

Several things can be said in reply to these objections. (1) This
separation of faith and history does violence to the very documents
which report the resurrection event. Time and time again the synop-
tic writers ground the teaching and preaching of the Word in the
historical event. In John the author takes pains to correlate particular
discourses with Jewish feasts, so as to give theological significance to
Jesus' utterances.[5] Peter's first sermon, as recorded in Acts, presents
the historical events of miracles and signs as attestations of God's
approval of Christ.[6] Paul, particularly in the passage under consideration, clearly connects the doctrine of immortality with historical reality, by appealing to the testimony of witnesses.[7]

The critics themselves recognize that this is the case. With respect to the resurrection of Jesus, Bultmann writes,

> Yet it cannot be denied that the resurrection of Jesus is often used in the
> New Testament as a miraculous proof. Take for instance Acts 17:31.
> Here we are actually told that God substantiated the claims of Christ by
> raising him from the dead. Then again the resurrection narratives: both
> the legend of the empty tomb and the appearances insist on the physical
> reality of the risen body of the Lord.[8]

Yet this primary testimony is rejected. On what grounds does
Bultmann do this? He suggests four. First, Bultmann rejects the claims
of the New Testament documents that faith is attested by historical
and empirical evidence on the ground that these passages are later
additions, and consequently do not provide us with an accurate understanding of the original kerygma and what really occurred. They
are later embellishments of the primitive tradition which reflect the
Church's reinterpretation of the life and ministry of Jesus of Nazareth
in light of new problems and questions facing the Church. Why does

Bultmann decide that these passages (particularly the ones dealing with the historicity of Jesus' resurrection) do not reflect the original kerygma? The reason given is that St. Paul, whose writings reflect the earlier tradition, knows nothing about the stories of the empty tomb and appearances. But though St. Paul does not refer directly to any of these stories, he certainly was not silent on the reality of the resurrection as a physical event, as Bultmann goes on to admit. In I Corinthians 15, St. Paul himself claims that Jesus was raised from the dead and adduces witnesses to establish the historicity of that resurrection.

Bultmann rejects or by-passes this passage on the grounds that adducing eye-witnesses "is a dangerous procedure. . . . An historical fact which involves a resurrection from the dead is utterly inconceivable."[9] The reason given here is an a priori one: resurrections are mythical events which just cannot occur. But that this is false should be clear from what we have said in chapters three and five, where we have shown that no matter what view of man one adopts, man can be immortal. There is nothing intrinsically impossible or inherently contradictory about the notion of personal immortality.

It is interesting and informative to note that in rejecting the testimony of the Gospels and Acts grounding faith on history, he appeals to the lack of notation in other documents, notably St. Paul. But when it is pointed out that Paul himself treats the matter in a similar way, Bultmann retreats to philosophical objections against the entire notion of resurrection. This retreat reveals the patently circular reasoning which lies at the foundation of his first argument. He rejects the testimony of the documents which establishes that faith is attested by the historical fact of the physical resurrection of Jesus on the grounds that it represents later additions and interpretations. And he decides that these are later additions on the grounds that they treat the resurrection as a physical event and adduce historical fact to justify faith. But this kind of argumentation provides no grounds for rejecting the testimony of the documents or their claim that faith can be attested by historical fact.

Thirdly, he rejects the New Testament's grounding of faith on history on the grounds that we cannot establish the objective historicity of most of the events in the New Testament, including the resurrection of Jesus. If we were to ground faith on history, we would be unable to account for the dynamic faith of Christianity, which possesses a paucity of historical evidence. Christian faith develops despite historical ignorance. However, I believe that he is mistaken in his assessment of the historical evidence relating to Christian faith. I shall attempt to support this contention in the following sections in detail with respect to the resurrection.

Fourthly, he states that the resurrection is an article of faith, and that one cannot prove one article of faith (for example, the redemptive aspect of the cross, or personal immortality) by appeal to another article of faith (the resurrection of Jesus). Why is the latter an article of faith? Because the resurrection is an eschatological event. That is, it has theological and existential significance for my present existence; by it death is overcome and we walk in newness of life. But surely, that an event has eschatological significance does not entail that the event does not likewise have historical significance. To reduce one to the other, or to reject the one altogether, is to miss the total significance of the event. It is to fail to see that the event contains a complex of historical and eschatological significances, and that if the event had not historically occurred, in all probability the eschatological significance would not have arisen. This seems particularly true in the case involving the resurrection of Jesus, where something had to happen to the disciples in order to change them from frightened, fleeing individuals to fearless preachers of the resurrection of Jesus.

In short, none of the reasons advanced by Bultmann provides grounds for rejecting the thesis of the documents that historical fact can be adduced to support existential faith. Indeed, to adopt this Bultmannian position is to destroy the very structure of Apostolic Christianity. Peter's and Paul's kerygma is that Jesus has been raised from the dead. But if the actual event of the resurrection is unimportant or of no consequence, does it any longer mean anything to say that Jesus is risen? The kerygma of Peter and Paul is turned into a Christ-myth, for their preaching has been divorced from the event which they proclaimed. Their claim is that faith in Jesus as actually risen is central to the Christian message, and that the resurrection provides God's attestation to Christ's ministry. To deny this claim as literal fact is to abandon the Apostolic Faith.

The kerygma of the first-century church is connected with historical factors. The acts of God in history, the birth, life, death, and resurrection of Jesus, all supply a ground or basis of faith. There is an integral connection between the kerygmatic Christ and activity of God, and the historical Jesus and salvation-events. Christian faith is faith not only in the Christ of the preached word, but also in the historical Jesus who died, was resurrected, and lives today. It is faith not only in the Easter of the kerygma, but in the resurrection of Jesus of Nazareth which is the subject of the kerygma. The connection between these is not accidental or unimportant, but essential to faith. St. Paul writes, "If Christ has not been raised, then our kerygma is in vain and your faith is in vain. We are even found to be misrepresenting God, because we testified of God that he raised Christ. . . . If Christ has not been raised, your faith is futile and you are still in your sins."[10] And the context makes it perfectly clear that it is the historical event which Paul has in mind.

Often it is difficult to understand what theologians really mean when they affirm that Jesus was raised from the dead but that this statement makes no historical or factual claim. Some, like Willi Marxsen, have attempted to give this meaning by distinguishing between two emphases contained within the statement, "Jesus is risen." On the one hand, the stress lies on the present. "Jesus is not a figure belonging to the past; he is not a dead person but a living one. Jesus lives. He is of vital concern to me personally." On the other hand, "the stress can equally well lie on the past. In this case our sentence means, roughly speaking: the crucified Jesus is risen in the sense that after three days he rose from the dead. This happened two thousand years ago. In this case the sentence does not primarily express a personal involvement on the part of the Christian; it is simply something known to the speaker."[11] After making this distinction, these writers attempt to argue that Christians can affirm the first meaning without coming to an agreement about what is meant in the second by "risen" or by "alive." That is, a Christian can "express his involvement" by saying that Jesus is of vital concern to him here and now, and that he is concerned with furthering Jesus' teaching and ministry, while at the same time affirming that Jesus is dead in an historical sense.[12] To say that Jesus is risen is simply one way of saying "he still comes to us today," that he (Jesus) is present in his offer of helping us to love our neighbor and rely on God. By acknowledging that Jesus is risen, we acknowledge the miracle of finding faith, that Jesus' past is present, and that he is present in the preaching of his offer.

But though one might legitimately distinguish between these two emphases of the statement "Jesus is risen," they cannot be separated, as Marxsen himself affirms. Neither can the statement make literal sense unless Jesus actually did come back to life. To attempt to give meaning to this statement by such reinterpretations as "my finding of faith is a miracle," "Jesus is present in the word of the proclamation," "the cause of Jesus continues," "the offer he made is still valid,"[13] while at the same time holding that Jesus is actually historically dead, is to confuse the statement "Jesus is risen (alive today)" with the statement "Jesus' influence continues today." To state that his ministry and teaching are still active in the hearts and lives of men, to say that his teachings provide a guide to my conduct, to say that through the preaching of Jesus I find faith and meaning, are quite different from saying that Jesus himself as a person is still alive. This, I trust, was made clear in chapter two, where we attempted to distinguish between immortality as remembrance and personal immortality. It is inappropriate and (perhaps intentionally) misleading to say "Jesus is risen" when one really means that his teachings are promulgated and followed or that his *influence* persists. In short, it is true that there are two stresses to the statement: a personal confession of faith and an historical statement. But one should not make the confession that Jesus is risen and alive unless one holds that it is an historical fact that he was raised and that he lives. If one means that he is dead, and that only his influence persists, then one should say so, and not couch it in traditional resurrection language. To circumvent this by "reinterpretative language" is, I believe, dishonest.

(2) What can be said about the objectors' contention that to adopt this view of the relation of faith to history destroys both the nature and the venture-aspect of faith? They are correct, I believe, when they contend that faith is the response of an individual to another individual or to a certain state of affairs. Faith is the act of commitment which appropriates the advances of the other to oneself, involving the implementation by one's entire being of what one believes. But this commitment or action can itself be reasonable or unreasonable. To commit oneself to an individual who has continually violated one's previous trust is to act irrationally. To act upon a certain set of beliefs which are demonstrably or even probably false is to act foolishly. For example, to set sail and make lengthy preparations for falling off the end of the earth might be called faith (that the world is flat), but surely it is an example of irrational and misguided faith.

The belief structure which underlies the faith should be open to objective scrutiny. If that belief structure is reasonable, if the data contained therein can be shown to be true or probably true, then it is reasonable to act upon (to have faith in) these beliefs. If, on the other hand, that belief structure can be shown to contain false assertions, then it is irrational faith to act upon or commit oneself on the basis of that belief structure. To be reasonable, a faith should be subject to objective scrutiny by both believer and unbeliever.

This by no means entails that my faith is subject to the controls of others. The *rationality* of my faith is dependent upon the knowledge and information compiled, regardless of who compiles it. But the act of commitment involved in the faith, the giving of meaning to my own existence, depends upon my own initiative. Merely because I know something does not mean that I have faith in it, that I am willing to commit myself to it or on the basis of it. Faith does not follow automatically from understanding. Rather, faith depends upon understanding to make itself reasonable. Personal initiative is called for in rational faith.

Does this then mean that there is no venture involved in the act of commitment? Certainly not. As we have already argued, knowledge only rarely yields certainty, and historical knowledge presents nothing more than probability. Thus, to act on the basis of probability is still to venture oneself on the sea of existence. All the factors bearing on the case are not known; that which will affect my action is, in part, still in the future, and to the extent that my action relates to others, undetermined. There remains risk, albeit a reasonable risk, and challenge in the action, for in the performance I am risking myself. Hence, the act of faith is a venture. And if the act can be shown to be a reasonable one, it is a reasonable venture, but a venture of my being-in-the-world nonetheless.

Is the Resurrection an Historical Event?

(3) If we are correct in our analysis of faith, then we must turn our attention to the third objection presented above, namely, that the historian cannot arrive at a determination of the historicity of the resurrection. The resurrection of Jesus of Nazareth, the objector argues, is at best an interpretation of certain reports or observed events, and at worst, a legend or myth created by men who were prone to believing in such. In either case, this alleged event is incapable of

providing the ground for an eschatological hope of personal immortality.

That there was an historical resurrection is not directly accessible to us today, for it is something which happened in history. Hence, we cannot use present experience to prove or disprove the claims that Jesus actually came out of the tomb. To discover whether the resurrection of Jesus was an historical event, we must go through others. And to do this we must employ the documents which first make this claim.

However, this procedure itself is not free from difficulties, for none of the writers of the New Testament documents was a witness to the event of the resurrection. Indeed, *no one* witnessed the resurrection event. From whence, then, did those writers derive their account? What was the basis of their belief? For the earliest believers it was the result of a process of inference. And for the New Testament writers, it was either again a process of inference based on their own experience, or a reception and enlarging of a tradition which had been passed down to them, depending on whether one accepts Matthew and John as the authors of the Gospels attributed to them. In either case, if we are to penetrate to the actual historical data, to discover what in fact occurred, we cannot simply adopt the beliefs of the New Testament writers, for their beliefs were a result of reflection; though, for that matter, neither can we ignore their claims. If we are to resolve the question of whether the resurrection was an actual historical event, we must begin by asking how the writers arrived at this belief, and whether their inference that Jesus was actually raised is a reasonable and reliable one.

The inference that was made was based upon an interpretation of two sorts of data, the empty tomb and the post-burial appearances of Jesus. Let us consider first the claim that the tomb was empty.

The Empty Tomb

The unanimous agreement of the New Testament writers that the tomb was found empty on that first Easter appears, at first sight, to provide affirmative evidence that here we are dealing with a primary given. However, such is not the universal opinion. For example, the contemporary German theologian Willi Marxsen contends that though we can be sure that the writers believed that the witnesses themselves believed that the tomb was empty, that is not in and of itself sufficient to enable us to affirm that the tomb really was empty. We cannot believe that such and such was the case merely because others believed that it was so. Rather, we must discover why the New Testament writers maintained this position.

Marxsen contends that we cannot, in this matter at least, get behind the writers.[14] That is, we cannot discover what the facts are concerning the tomb of Jesus, for the accounts of the empty tomb are not found in but are later additions to the earliest accounts. To support this contention he appeals to a number of apparent inconsistencies between the reports. First, how many women came that first Easter morning? Were there two as in Matthew, three as in Mark, a number as in Luke, or only Mary Magdalene as in John? Secondly, why did the women come to the tomb? Matthew reports that they wanted to see the tomb, while Mark and Luke report that they wanted to anoint the body with spices. But either they wanted to see the tomb, or else they wanted to anoint the body. Thirdly, Matthew reports that an earthquake occurred while the women were at the site; the other reporters know nothing of it. But either the stone was rolled away in their presence by heavenly intervention, or else they found the stone already rolled away. Fourthly, did they see an angel (Matthew), a young man (Mark), or two men (Luke)? Were these individuals inside the tomb (Mark), seated on the stone (Matthew), or standing nearby (Luke)? Fifthly, in Matthew and Mark the women are told to convey to the disciples the message that Jesus would meet them in Galilee. Luke, however, transforms this command into a reminiscence of Jesus' teaching in Galilee, where he had promised that he would rise from the dead. Finally, did they tell no one because they were afraid (Mark), or did they go and repeat their story to the disciples (Matthew and Luke)?

These apparent inconsistencies, Marxsen contends, indicate not only that these accounts were not part of the earliest tradition and were added by the writers themselves to answer current objections to their ministry (as with Matthew's account of the stationing of the Roman guard at the tomb), but also that the writers themselves were not concerned with the historical reality of the empty tomb, but rather with its meaning and function. That is, the story of the empty tomb is a form of kerygma used to convey the idea that Jesus' work continues. If they had been concerned with the resurrection and empty tomb as an historical event, there would be uniform accounts.[15]

However, I believe that a sympathetic reading of the documents will show that these inconsistencies are only apparent. First, as to who visited the tomb that morning, Luke informs his readers that there were a number of women besides the ones he names. Thus, though each author names or focuses on a few, this does not indicate that his listing conflicts with other listings, for who they listed depended on who was there, on their knowledge of the event, and the interests of themselves and their readers. An analogous situation might be the reports of those who attended the funeral of Martin Luther King. Although there were many other individuals in attendance, each of the news services gave its own listing of certain dignitaries. Though the lists differ and are not complete, that does not mean that they are not and were not meant to be accurate accounts of the event of the funeral or of who was in attendance. Their listing was dictated by space and special interests, as well as by who was there.

Secondly, it is specious to suggest a conflict between wanting to see the tomb and wanting to anoint the body. Certainly the visitors' motivation for coming was complex, particularly since more than one woman was involved.

Thirdly, the passage in Matthew indicates that the soldiers and women were frightened not by the earthquake, but by the appearance of the young man at the tomb. Indeed, Matthew does not specifically state that the earthquake occurred while the women were at the tomb. Hence there is no inconsistency involved in the stories which recount their procession to the tomb, the occurrence of an earthquake, the discovery of the removed stone, and the appearance of the young man to them upon their arrival at the tomb.

Fourthly, Luke uses both the terms "men" and "angels." There is no contradiction here: what they saw were men whom they took or interpreted to be angels. And further, there is no reason to think that these men had to stay in one place all the time, that they could not move around both inside and outside the tomb.

Fifthly, the message conveyed to the women could have contained both a reminder of prophecies made during Jesus' ministry and an indication of where they were to meet him. That Luke stresses the prophetic aspect does not entail that he changed the instructive into the prophetic. Indeed, due to the unusual circumstances and the state of mind of the women, undoubtedly the message was repeated several times, probably in slightly differing forms.

Finally, the women were at first filled with mixed emotions.

They were both joyous at this sudden turn of events, and afraid that what they saw and heard was not true. Accordingly, at first they resolved not to tell anyone, as indicated by Mark. But then, as Matthew records, Jesus met them. They recognized him and sought to worship him. After he reiterated the same message, they were sure that he had indeed risen, and hurried off to tell the disciples. Thus, the complexity of the event and of the emotions experienced by the women is fully apparent from a comparison of the texts, and the seeming contradiction disappears.

From the documents we can thus develop a consistent account. On the first day of the week a number of women met together, while it was still dark (before daybreak), to make the short trip to the tomb of Jesus, some to see it for the first time, others to anoint the body if possible. On their way an earthquake occurred, rolling the stone from the doorway. When they arrived after daybreak, they saw a man seated on the tombstone. Though frightened by his speech and appearance, the women entered the tomb; but Mary Magdalene ran to tell Peter and the other disciple that someone had removed the stone and the body. On entering, the women saw both that the body was removed and that another man was present. The men told them (undoubtedly more than once) that Jesus had risen as he promised, and that they were to convey a message to his disciples. They left the tomb with mixed emotions, both fearing and rejoicing, but at first were too frightened to tell anyone. However, Jesus himself met them and reiterated the command. Recovering from their fear, they separated (since the disciples were probably scattered throughout the area, living with friends) and ran to tell the disciples what they had experienced. Meanwhile, Peter and the other disciple ran to the tomb, followed by Mary Magdalene.

Though this is perhaps not the only way the material can be consistently organized, it does serve to show that from a sympathetic reading of the partial accounts a consistent story can be developed, and that there is no reason to suppose that these are later additions or that the writers were not interested in reporting what actually occurred. Indeed, all else aside, there is total agreement on the particular aspect with which we are here concerned: that the tomb was empty and the announcement made that Jesus was risen. Likewise, there is specific interest shown in confirming the vacancy of the tomb. The writers emphasize that the women themselves looked into and entered the tomb, and that Peter and the other disciple, upon hearing that the tomb was empty, ran to and entered the tomb to confirm it. The historicity of the empty tomb is clearly in view.

Granted, then, that there is reasonably good historical evidence to show that the tomb was empty; what does this tell us about the resurrection of Jesus? The empty tomb itself, Marxsen contends, tells us nothing about Jesus' resurrection. Not only does it fail to inform us as to how the resurrection took place or what the resurrection body was like,[16] but it likewise leaves open the question of whether the resurrection took place at all. If all we had was the empty tomb, Marxsen argues, we would certainly have no *proof* of the resurrection.

> Now if I mention Jesus' resurrection in connexion with the empty tomb, then "the resurrection of Jesus" is an interpretation and is intended to explain the existence of the fact that the tomb was empty. It is therefore not permissible (in connexion with the story about the empty tomb) to speak of the *event* of Jesus' resurrection, because it is not permissible to turn an interpretation into an objective fact; it is quite obvious that the empty tomb (even if its historical truth could be successfully proved) would be in no way a "proof"[17] of Jesus' resurrection.[18]

That it is not a proof must be granted because the absence of the physical body from the garden tomb is not a sufficient condition for the resurrection of Jesus, for the absence of the physical body is a fact that could be interpreted in a number of different ways. For example, the disciples could have stolen the body, a gardener could have spirited it away, Jesus' enemies could have secretly removed and interred the body, or Jesus' body could have been restored to life. Indeed, Matthew clearly indicates that at the time he wrote his Gospel there were in existence at least two differing accounts of the empty tomb.

However, though Marxsen is correct in his contention that by itself the disappearance of the body proves nothing about the resurrection, I believe that he is mistaken in concluding from this that the term "event" is not applicable to the resurrection of Jesus. Without going into detail, I believe that he has confused several different senses of "interpretation" in his article. The sense of "interpretation" we are most concerned with is the sense of "hypothesis": which hypothesis will best explain the observed facts. But an hypothesis, if true, does itself report a fact. The difference between the hypothesis and the evidence is not that one is a fact and the other is not or cannot be one. It is a difference in our knowledge of the situation: we know the evidence; we infer the hypothesis. Therefore, whichever hypothesis is the true one represents the state of affairs which obtained, and hence expresses an event. If the true hypothesis was that Jesus was resurrected, then Jesus' resurrection was an event.

Returning to the empty tomb, we have a fact which needs explanation. However, standing by itself, this fact can be explained by a number of differing hypotheses. Which is the correct one must be determined by appeal to other facts, facts which will tend to confirm some hypotheses and refute others.

In summary, that the tomb was empty is a statement about a certain state of affairs which in principle was observable and verifiable at the time when the women witnessed the event, though obviously not so now. That the stone was rolled from the doorway, that there was no body inside, that someone spoke to them, are matters of direct observation on their part. Moreover, it is clear that these events are reported by the writers with an eye toward their historicity. Pains are taken to stress that the women observed the empty tomb, that they entered it, and that other disciples checked it out. Indeed, that the story appears first in the resurrection accounts shows the importance attached to it.

However, to account for the fact of the empty tomb, interpretation, or, better, an hypothesis, is needed. Indeed, the writers of the accounts themselves recognize this, for this is precisely the function of the young men at the tomb. But since several different hypotheses are viable explanations of the fact that the tomb was empty, we need to turn to the other area of corroborating evidence from which the witnesses and writers made their inference that Jesus was risen. In this way we can substantially reduce the number of reasonable alternative hypotheses.

The Appearances of Jesus

When we turn to the reports of the appearances of Jesus to his disciples and others, many of the same issues which we have just developed with respect to the empty tomb again arise. On the one hand, the documents are unanimous in their report that the Jesus who was crucified appeared bodily to a variety of witnesses. They stress both his physical existence and his personal identity with the one who died.

For example, to convince Thomas the doubter, Jesus is pictured as presenting wounds of his crucifixion and lancing.

On the other hand, many individuals have manifested scepticism over the appearance reports, arguing that they cannot form part of the early tradition, but must be later additions. The elaborate tales are literary developments of vision reports. Two sorts of evidence for this contention are introduced.[19] First, it is felt that the various accounts depicting Jesus' resurrection body are not easily reconcilable. At times, it is presented in highly material terms: Jesus eats, he can be touched, his wounds are visible; at other times it is presented as spiritual: he appears and disappears suddenly and at will, he moves through closed doors. In addition, his disciples and Mary Magdalene had difficulty recognizing him, and doubts about his identity continued to crop up in succeeding days. These conflicting motifs indicate that the New Testament writers were *not* concerned with the resurrection body as an historical object and hence with the resurrection as an historical event.

Secondly, they contend that it is impossible to harmonize the various accounts of the appearances of Jesus. First, Matthew and John report that Jesus appeared to two and one woman respectively; this is contradicted by Luke, who states that the disciples on the Emmaus road told their unrecognized companion that no one had seen Jesus (24:24). Secondly, the accounts given by Luke and John of the appearance of Jesus to the disciples in a Jerusalem house contain differing features.

> The would-be harmonizer will hardly be inclined to maintain that there were two different appearances. But if there was only one, who reports it correctly? Were the disciples first doubtful (Luke) or were they immediately overjoyed (John)? What were the words with which Jesus sent the disciples forth? Did Jesus breathe on them, giving them the gift of the Holy Spirit (John), or not (Luke)?[20]

Further, John records that Thomas was absent at the first meeting, whereas Luke indicates that all eleven disciples were present at that first meeting. Finally, there appear to be serious conflicts between the Judean appearances and ascension account given in Luke and John, and the Galilean appearances recorded in Matthew and John. The order in which these events occurred, it is claimed, is difficult if not impossible to determine. Moreover, why does the missionary charge have to be repeated in Galilee if it had already been given to the disciples in Jerusalem?

This indicates, the critic argues, that the Gospel writers were not concerned to develop an historical account of what happened, that is, an account for the sake of simply recording what transpired. Rather, they were concerned for the *function* of any account that they might construct. And what was that function? They were concerned to show that the activity of Jesus still goes on and that the disciples had a fundamental role to play in continuing his mission. The priority of Peter and the authority of the Apostles had to be established. Justification had to be given for the global expanse of the Gospel to the Gentiles. Consequently, the writers depicted or reconstructed the events as they best fit into this schema or best advanced this justification. Thus we can explain the priority assigned to Peter in Jesus' order of appearances in Luke and John and the frequently given missionary charges.

As with the empty tomb, if the writers had been concerned with the historicity of the resurrection appearances, they would have sought to develop consistent and unified accounts of the appearances. Rather, all that we are provided with is a number of conflicting and fragmentary accounts.

However, here again a sympathetic reading of the documents provides the possibility of reconciling these apparent inconsistencies and developing from the partial accounts a coherent though necessarily incomplete story of the appearances of Jesus. Turning first of all to the alleged inconsistencies with respect to Jesus' resurrection body, the documents present elements which are both similar to and different from his previous mode of existence. He ate broiled fish; he could be touched; he possessed the wounds inflicted on the cross. Yet he had additional powers or abilities to appear or disappear suddenly or to pass through closed doors. But there is nothing inherently contradictory about this complex of properties. It is true that the latter are not normally associated with bodies as known to us. But merely because they are not part of our ordinary or common experience does not entail that they are incompatible properties of any physical or bodily object. To take just one example, most of us have seen pictures of hay straws which have been thrust unbroken through wooden telephone poles by tornado winds. It is true that this is not normally possible; if we attempted to push a straw through the pole, it would break. But this does serve to show that there is nothing inherently contradictory about a physical object passing unharmed through another physical object. In both cases, that the objects involved were physical is not contradicted by the event in question. What is indicated in both cases is that additional causal factors or laws were involved.

The documents do not intend to give an exhaustive philosophical or scientific account of the nature of Jesus' resurrection body. They merely report events as witnessed by certain individuals. That those events indicate that the post-resurrection composition or powers of his body were different from those of the pre-resurrection body in certain respects does not entail confusion on the part of the writers or witnesses. It is highly parochial to suggest that such a body, even a physical one, could not possess characteristics other than those possessed in pre-resurrection experience, especially since we have no personal experience with resurrection bodies.

Secondly, what can be said about the alleged inconsistencies between the various resurrection accounts? First, Matthew's and John's reports of Jesus' appearances to the women are not contradicted by Luke. Luke does not recount that the Emmaus disciples said that no one had seen Jesus. Rather, they reputedly stated that the *disciples* (or better, "those among us") *who went to the tomb* did not see Jesus, which furthermore correlates with Luke's statement about Peter (24:12) and John's report of the race between Peter and the other disciple to the tomb (20:3-8).

Secondly, the accounts of Luke and John describing the appearance of Jesus to the disciples in the Jerusalem house are not as disparate as supposed. Luke states that they first were afraid, but then rejoiced when Jesus identified himself by the demonstration of his wounds, though their rejoicing and gladness were still tempered with lingering doubts. John omits the first part, but hints that this was the initial reaction, since he likewise stresses Jesus' act of self-identification. There is no contradiction involved in the disciples entertaining a number of emotions. It is the mixed emotions of fear and joy, of doubt and hope, which are here in sight and which it is a mistake to oversimplify. It is a simplistic psychology indeed which condemns the disciples to only one emotion at a time. Moreover, Jesus undoubtedly said many things to them in that room. There is no reason to think that he could not have repeated his missionary command to them several times, in different ways. Indeed, recalling the success of his past teachings, as manifested by the disciples' reaction in the garden, it was probably necessary. Part of this commissioning involved the "endowment" with the Spirit. In Luke we are made aware that the disciples will not be left alone, but that they will receive that which was promised by the Father, that is, the Spirit. The breathing of Jesus upon the assembled, recorded by John, can be understood as a sign or symbol of what was to come, for the Spirit would be the breath *(pneuma)* of Christ and God. But it was only a foretaste and not the full endowment. This is made clear elsewhere in John, where Jesus states that the Spirit could not come until Christ was taken from them (7:39; 16:7).

Thirdly, a conflict is seen between Luke's record that the Emmaus disciples returned to Jerusalem, and met with "the eleven," and John's record that Thomas was absent, leaving only ten present. However, the use of "the eleven" here could be interpreted as parallel to uses of such terms as "the twelve," "the Congress," "the 450 delegates," and so on. It might be said that the Congress was assembled to hear the President's State of the Union address, but that certain individual members were absent. In similar fashion, the term "twelve" is used by Paul in I Corinthians 15:5; Christ is said to have appeared to the twelve, indicating the *group* to which he appeared, though in fact Judas was dead. Similarly, "the eleven" here could indicate the group present, and not the number.

Finally, was it impossible or unlikely that Jesus met with his disciples both in Jerusalem and in Galilee?

> Is it, after all, so impossible for holders of an "objective" view to conceive of appearances taking place first in Jerusalem and then in Galilee — and, possibly, then once again in Jerusalem? The Eleven were all, it seems, Galileans. Therefore they were in Judea only as pilgrims for the Passover Festival, as Jesus himself had been. Within a short time (say, a week) of the end of the Festival, they would naturally return to their homes in Galilee. Why should it be impossible — if they really saw Jesus at all — that some of them, at least, should see him first in Jerusalem, and then in Galilee? Again . . . there is no intrinsic reason why the appearances should not have extended over an appreciable length of time. And, if so, why should not some of them have taken place at Jerusalem again *after* the forty or fifty days separating Passover from the next Pilgrim Feast, Pentecost, for which the disciples might have gone up to Jerusalem once more?[21]

Here again, then, it seems that the objection of inconsistency can be met and a consistent story developed from the texts, such that there is no reason why one must conclude that the appearance stories either were later additions to the earlier traditions or were not meant to report what actually occurred. It is of course true that none of the authors presents a complete account, but lack of completeness does not entail or even indicate disinterest in reporting events as they occurred. Indeed, all else aside, there is total agreement on the particular aspect with which we are here concerned: that the witnesses did see Jesus after his death and burial. Further, there is specific interest shown in verifying that this one who appeared to them was identical with the one who died and was buried. The writers emphasize that he showed them his crucifixion wounds and recounted past events and discourses.

Much has been made of the subsequent and lingering doubts of the disciples. This has been interpreted to mean that the one who appeared was not really recognizable, and hence it could have been another individual. But the instances of the witnesses' failure to immediately identify Jesus are not mystifying or unexplainable. Mary Magdalene was weeping and probably not even looking at the "gardener" who approached her. The disciples who were fishing at dawn were a distance offshore and hence had difficulty recognizing a dimly lit figure standing on the beach. And finally, this entire resurrection experience was a difficult one for them to comprehend and believe; this accounts for their mixed emotions of both joy and doubt upon Jesus' appearance to them in the Jerusalem house. In any case, their subsequent actions and ministry can leave no doubt that they were finally and incontrovertibly convinced that the one who appeared to them was really the risen Lord.

Granted, then, that we have good historical evidence for the witnesses' claim that after his death Jesus appeared to them, what does this tell us about the resurrection of Jesus? Here again the witnesses had to make an inference based on certain evidence. The evidence was that the tomb was empty and that an individual who appeared to be the same Jesus who was crucified was now conversing and eating with them. Some sort of inference had to be drawn, some sort of hypothesis advanced. And which hypothesis would best explain these events? Surely the hypotheses that the disciples stole the body or that the theft was committed by their enemies or an unscrupulous gardener no longer held. The most reasonable hypothesis for *these witnesses* was that Jesus had been raised from the dead. This would best account for the empty tomb and his living presence with them, though, as can be seen from the texts, they were slow to adopt it, probably because such an event was so contrary to their normal experience and expectations.

The same, I think, can be said for the writers of the Gospels. Insofar as they sought to compile a narrative of the things which had been accomplished among them and accepted what was delivered to them by eye-witnesses and preachers of the tradition (Luke 1:1-4), they recorded the interpretations of these early traditions. Insofar as they themselves drew conclusions based upon the evidence presented to them, they too saw this hypothesis as the most reasonable one, and hence concluded that Jesus had been raised from the dead.

Moreover, even if they did have purposes other than the mere recounting of events, as seems evident, that does not mean that they created or fictionalized the events to suit their own purposes. Their purposes were several. They wanted to demonstrate that the activity of Jesus continues through the mission of the Church. They desired to provide a justification for the global proclamation and inclusiveness of the Gospel. They wanted to explain the priority of Peter and the authority of the Apostles. The answering of the critics did play a part in what they considered significant in the traditions passed down to them. Yet each and all of these are perfectly consistent with a report of the events as they occurred. What they provide is the basis of selection, whereby the writers chose from among the traditions of what occurred that which they felt was important to recount. In short, plurality of purposes provides a selectivity factor; the pool which is selected from is the oral and written traditions of what occurred.

Application to the Question of the Historicity of the Resurrection

With this, let us now return to the issues posed when we took up the question whether the resurrection is an historical event. There we noted that since the primary resurrection evidence is not accessible to us today, we must employ the testimony of others, and in particular, the testimony of the New Testament writers. But to discover the primary historical ground we cannot simply accept what the writers said about the events which they experienced or which they reported others to have experienced. We must understand how they arrived at their report. And that understanding must take account of the inferences which were drawn, both by the original witnesses and the writers. We have now seen what those inferences were and why they were drawn. The events experienced and reported to the writers could best be explained by the hypothesis that Jesus had actually risen. Moreover, we have also seen that part of their reason for reporting these events was to let the reader know what had actually occurred. This is evident both from their own explanation of what they were doing and from their manner of presenting the material. For example, the witnesses are presented as checking out their experiences, both by making special trips to verify that the tomb was empty, and by seeking physical proof from the one who appeared, that he was identical with the crucified Jesus.

But what about us? Do we have good grounds for stating, as the original witnesses and authors did, that Jesus was raised from the dead? Marxsen contends that the empty tomb and appearance reports do not prove that the resurrection is an historical event. Though the witnesses were certainly speaking of events which they believed were real,

> we are no longer in a position to speak so directly of the resurrection of Jesus as an *event*; we must simply say: *We are concerned with an interpretative statement* made use of by those who reflected on what had happened to them (at that time!). Hence if today we raise the question in *historical* terms (!): Is Jesus risen? — we can only reply: That cannot be established. *In historical terms it can only be established* (though quite reliably) that witnesses, after the death of Jesus, claimed that something had happened to them which they described as seeing Jesus, and reflection on this experience led them to the *interpretation* that Jesus had been raised from the dead.[22]

Marxsen argues that today all we possess are the experience reports of the witnesses and their interpretations of what they claim to have experienced. But we are not in a position to have these experiences ourselves. Thus, the only thing with which we can be concerned is their interpretations. But interpretative statements do not report events. Therefore, we cannot make historical judgments about the resurrection.

If we generalize from this argument, it would seem that not only can we make no historical judgments about the particular issue under consideration, but we can make *no* historical judgments. If we reject this *kind* of data — reports of witnesses of their experiences — as providing *grounds* for making sound historical judgments, what kind of data could supply this ground? It is the very nature of historical data to consist of reports of events made by witnesses who claim to have experienced such and such. If we were allowed to make historical judgments only about what we ourselves experience, historical research and writing would become impossible.

Secondly, he contends that we cannot make an historical judgment because we are only concerned with interpretations, and these do not record events. We have responded to this above when we considered his evaluation of the empty tomb accounts. There we noted that the kind of interpretation we are concerned with is hypothesis, and that an hypothesis, if true, does record an event, and, if false, does not. Thus, in questioning about an hypothesis we are indeed concerned with whether or not a particular historical *event* occurred, and in affirming or denying such an hypothesis, making an historical judgment.

Marxsen has misunderstood the nature of historical evidence and inference. Thus he fails to see that we too possess evidence, indeed, much the same evidence that the Gospel writers had. We are not limited to a concern for interpretative statements. Like the original reporters, we too, as concerned with (among other questions) the question of the historicity of the event, are faced with the same need to evaluate the evidence and to make an historical inference based upon what we consider to be good evidence.

Indeed, to make our inference, not only do we have the reports of the early Christian tradition, giving us the grounds for the original belief, but we likewise have the witness of the lives of the disciples themselves. As has been noted by many, it is extremely difficult, if not impossible, to account for the sudden and dramatic change in the disciples simply by appealing to their subjective vision, or to a determination on their part to change their personalities and become proclaimers of the "dead" prophet. For example, G.W.H. Lampe writes,

> All the indications in the Gospels suggest that at the time of the arrest of Jesus the disciples lost all hope and faith in Jesus. They all forsook him and fled, except Peter, and he very soon denied all knowledge of him. Unless something extraordinary happened to convince them that against all their expectations God had reversed his apparent verdict on Jesus, I cannot imagine that they would later on have taken immense

risks to assert in public that a man who had been condemned and hanged was no less than God's Messiah. It proved difficult enough to persuade the world that this was so, even when it was proclaimed by men who believed that God had raised him from the dead.[23]

But it is precisely this change from fearing, fleeing men into fearless proclaimers that must be explained. The only reasonable explanation of this turnabout is that Jesus did rise from the dead, appeared to them, and personally conveyed to them his command. This is not to say that the appearances were sufficient to cause belief. Even these appearances seem not to have been enough for the disciples, for after receiving the missionary command from Jesus, they returned to their former occupation of fishing. There had to be a final, supernatural change, which Acts speaks of as the filling with the Spirit on Pentecost. But it is to say that unless they had truly experienced the living Jesus, such a radical change in their being-in-the-world cannot be satisfactorily explained.

Indeed, that this encounter best explains their radical change is confirmed by the preached message of these missionaries. Central to their message was the claim that the resurrection of Jesus was an historical event.

Thus, in asking the historical question, Is Jesus risen?, we are faced with a report of the facts (the empty tomb, the post-resurrection appearances, the radical change in the disciples) and with the explanation of these given by the witnesses and writers. But in making the historical judgment, we too must pass on the evidence and present a reasoned hypothesis which explains this evidence. We have tried to show that there is good reason to accept the evidence as given. Likewise, we have argued that there is good reason for making the same hypothesis which the early writers made to explain these events. It is true that this is not a proof of Jesus' resurrection; but then proof in historical matters is impossible to achieve. Likewise, it is true that it is an "interpretation" of certain given facts, but the hypothesis, if true, is as much a reporting of the facts of the case as is the statement of the evidence for that hypothesis. Thus, if our hypothesis is true, we can speak historically of the resurrection of Jesus as an event. Therefore, contrary to Marxsen and similar critics, there are good historical grounds for the historical statement that after his death Jesus was raised from the dead and that this resurrection is an historical *event*.

Conclusion

As we have seen, objectors to the historical-theological argument most frequently focus their criticism against either the manner in which the argument grounds the theological upon the historical or against the historical claims made by the argument. We not only have attempted to show that it is proper to ground the theological upon the historical, but have also suggested that the historicity of the event in question can be established with some degree of probability.

One question, however, remains. If the historical-theological argument requires the presence of theological assertions to interpret the historical event, is the historical really necessary to the conclusion? That is, does this argument provide anything more than would the mere theological assertion that God has revealed to man that he will confer immortality upon him? In both cases, it seems, we are grounding our belief in human immortality upon a theological assertion which we claim is a revelation from God.

It might be replied that there is a difference, and that the difference is that which exists between a mere assertion and an argument. With the one, there is no evidence to support the assertion; we must merely accept it as true. With the other, however, there is an appeal made to evidence to support the conclusion. In the argument given by St. Paul, the contention is both that if Christ was raised, we too shall be raised, and if he was not raised, neither will we be raised.

However, the question still remains, How do we know that the bi-implication is true? The grounds are theological; we accept it to be true because it is an item of divine revelation. But these grounds are no different from those given to support the assertion that God's promise of immortality to man is true.

Perhaps, then, the value of the argument lies not in giving a convincing proof to the non-believer, for the non-believer presumably would already have rejected the possibility of divine revelation, or at least the truth of the theological assertions involved. Rather its value is for the believer, for it provides for this individual a probabilistic guarantee of his own re-creation. Insofar as he accepts the fundamental implication — if Christ was raised, we shall be raised — as true, he can then more assuredly hold that the consequent is true by showing that the antecedent is true. That is, accepting the implication means that if there are grounds for believing that the antecedent is true, then the belief about our own re-creation is thereby strengthened.

How, then, are we to respond to our question, Are there any good reasons for maintaining that man is immortal? In the absence of sound, deductive arguments, the answer one gives, I believe, depends in part upon the particular view of man which one holds, and in part upon one's theological beliefs or disbeliefs. If one adopts the monistic view of man (or else a dualism where the soul is not the person and the body is a necessary condition for one's existence), it would appear that ultimately we are thrown back upon theological assumptions and divine revelation to establish personal immortality. Insofar as one accepts the existence of a God who can create and divine revelation of his promise to re-create us, there is good reason for holding that man is immortal, as we have just argued. Insofar as one rejects the existence of God or denies that God reveals his purposes, there would appear to be no reason to hold that man is immortal. Indeed, the evidence of universal human mortality and bodily corruption point in the opposite direction. Thus, for the monist personal immortality appears unlikely unless there is a God who can and will intervene.

If, on the other hand, one adopts the dualistic view of man which holds that the soul is the real person, the situation is different. The contrary evidence of universal human mortality and bodily corruption would not be relevant, for the soul, as non-physical, cannot be affected by them. As such, there is no reason to think that the soul does not persist through death. Hence, it would appear reasonable (though by no means the conclusion of a sound, deductive argument) to hold that man is immortal because of the nature of the soul, even if there is no God. Whether or not God is necessary on this view depends on whether one holds that each soul has always existed. Unless the soul has always existed, there must be some agent, non-physical like the soul, which can produce the soul and couple it with the earthly body.

NOTES

1. I Corinthians 15.

2. Willi Marxsen, *The Resurrection of Jesus of Nazareth* (Philadelphia: Fortress, 1970), p. 152.

3. Rudolph Bultmann, quoted in Carl Henry, *Frontiers in Modern Theology* (Chicago: Moody Press, 1966), p. 21.

4. Rudolph Bultmann, "New Testament and Mythology," *Kerygma and Myth,* ed. Hans Werner Bartsch (N.Y.: Harper and Row, 1961), p. 42.

5. John 6:4; 7:2.

6. Acts 2:22.

7. See also Acts 2:31; 3:15; 5:32; 10:39-41.

8. Bultmann, "New Testament and Mythology," *op. cit.,* p. 39.

9. *Ibid.*

10. I Corinthians 15:14-17.

11. Marxsen, *op. cit.,* p. 18.

12. *Ibid.,* p. 147.

13. *Ibid.,* pp. 141-148.

14. *Ibid.,* ch. 2.

15. *Ibid.,* pp. 68, 76-78.

16. *Ibid.,* p. 43.

17. Marxsen's talk about "proof" here in regard to the resurrection of Jesus is misleading and mistaken. There can be no definitive proof in historical matters; neither can there be proof of an hypothesis. Events confirm hypotheses, but the same event can confirm a number of different hypotheses. Thus, events cannot prove hypotheses. To attempt to use the term in this fashion is to be mistaken about the relation of hypothesis to fact.

18. Willi Marxsen, "The Resurrection of Jesus as a Historical and Theological Problem," *The Significance of the Message of the Resurrection for Faith in Jesus Christ,* ed. C.F.D. Moule (London: S.C.M. Press, 1968), p. 25.

19. Marxsen, *The Resurrection of Jesus of Nazareth,* ch. 2.

20. *Ibid.,* p. 73.

21. C.F.D. Moule, "Introduction," *Significance of the Message . . . ,* pp. 4-5. Reconciliation of the texts becomes easier if there is, as seems likely on present evidence, textual corruption at the end of Luke (24:51b and 52a are not present in some ancient manuscripts).

22. Marxsen, "The Resurrection of Jesus as . . . ," *op. cit.,* p. 31.

23. G.W.H. Lampe, "Easter: A Statement," *The Resurrection,* ed. William Purcell (Philadelphia: The Westminster Press, 1966), pp. 30-31.

CHAPTER NINE

Life After Death

IN THIS FINAL CHAPTER I INTEND TO CONSIDER BRIEFLY A question which, though not directly posed in our previous discussions, has been alluded to. That is, "What will be the nature of life after death?" If, as I have tried to show, it is reasonable to hold (though by no means certain) that an individual both can and will live subsequent to his death or the death of his body, one naturally wishes to discover what that existence will be like. Questions such as "What will I be able to perceive and know in that world?" "Will I be able to communicate with other individuals?" "Can I act in that world?" "Where will this Next World be?" become relevant and intriguing.

From the outset, in light of what we have said above, it should be obvious that the answers to these and other such questions depend upon the particular view of man adopted. More specifically, the kind of life anticipated for man conceived as a disembodied soul differs significantly from that for man conceived as an embodied soul or unified person. Whereas for the latter it would appear that present language and concepts would be appropriate to describe the state of life after death, such would not appear to be the case for the former. To describe the life of the disembodied soul, we must engage in a process of subtraction of predicates used in our present existence. In particular, we cannot use language which requires or refers to the presence and activity of the physical body. But if we subtract this from the description of one's manner or mode of existence, is it any longer meaningful to speak about the disembodied life of the individual human person after death?

Of course, it might be the case that the passage from embodied to disembodied existence involves more than mere subtraction, that it includes the endowment of the soul with new characteristics, abilities, powers, and dispositions, or liberates those already extant but largely unrecognized and undeveloped from the restraints imposed by the physical body. If this is so, projections from our present knowledge to the nature of this after-life could be grossly inaccurate. This is the risk we must take in trying to answer the questions posed, and the presence of this risk must make us constantly aware that what we say by way of description is limited to our present knowledge of human powers and abilities. However, we can proceed in no other way unless we choose to lapse into silence about the future, for in order to speak meaningfully *now* about the *Next* World, we must use the language and concepts of our present world.

In this chapter we shall take this risk in order to explore the questions posed above. We shall first consider what life after death might be like for man considered as a disembodied soul, and then for man considered as a re-created, embodied individual.

Life After Death for the Disembodied Soul

A belief commonly found in both Western and non-Western religions is that the individual human person exists after death (or more accurately, the death of the body) if not forever, at least for a time, in a disembodied state. If this be the kind of existence which characterizes the immortal individual, what can be said about the Next Life?

Clearly, anything which requires the presence and activity of the physical body must be eliminated from a description of this mode of existence. For instance, one cannot speak of the *perceptual activities* of seeing, hearing, feeling, tasting, and smelling, for these require the presence and activity of physical sense organs. Neither can one speak of *acts of agency* which would necessitate bodily activity, such as running to the grocery store or typing this page. Consequently, it would seem not to make sense to say that an individual after the death of his body sees what another person is doing, can observe events on earth, or can interfere with the physical world by lifting tables or moving furniture.

But perhaps this conclusion is too hastily drawn; maybe perception and agency can be accounted for without invoking the presence of the physical body. Taking *perception* first, one writer has attempted to make sense of perceptual predicates by interpreting perception in terms of having certain experiences. To say, for example, that a disembodied person sees something is to say that he has certain visual experiences. "A disembodied person might have a visual field in which the objects set before him were arranged in the pattern in which they would be arranged for a normal observer in optimum circumstances viewing these objects from a particular position in space."[1] Similarly with the other perceptual senses; the disembodied person could have auditory, tactile, taste, and olfactory experiences insofar as he experienced sounds, textures, tastes, and so on which a normal individual would experience were he located at a given place. The presence of these experiences would constitute what we would mean by the statement, "The disembodied individual perceives in such and such a mode (sees, hears, etc.)."

But is this an adequate account of perception? Take the case of seeing as having visual experiences. For one thing, how would this act of seeing differ from hallucinating, dreaming, or imagining? Hallucination likewise involves experiencing a visual field with objects arranged perspectivally in a certain pattern. If the hallucination were a particularly convincing one, they would be arranged as they would be for a normal observer. This analysis would reduce seeing, hallucinating, dreaming, and imagining to the same thing: having visual experiences. For another thing, seeing, as a perceptual act, involves more than merely entertaining a visual field or having a visual experience. It is something that one does with one's body. That sensory perception is a bodily act becomes clearer when we consider the other perceptual senses of taste and touch. The reason these cases are clearer on this point is that perceptual acts involving these senses leave a mark on the object perceived, which is not the case with hearing, seeing, or smelling. A fingerprint is stamped on the glass; the orange rind becomes wet with saliva or bears evidence of mastication. These marks are indicative of the fact that these perceptual acts are bodily acts. But a disembodied being cannot leave fingerprints or secrete saliva. Thus, it would not make sense to say that it could perceive by tasting and touching; correspondingly, it would be meaningless to say that it could see, hear, or smell.

The apparent source of Penelhum's mistake is that his analysis of perception deals only with the product or result of the act of, for example, seeing (that is, the visual experience), but ignores the process which produces that effect. The disembodied soul can have a visual image of a certain figure-ground configuration, and this might even be an accurate representation of the true state of affairs as seen by a normal observer from a particular perspective. But the having of a visual image is no more seeing than remembering, imagining, or hallucinating. It is merely the product of seeing (and of a number of other processes as well), not the process of seeing. It is because Penelhum has confused product with process that he can say that it is meaningful to ascribe perceptual predicates to disembodied souls.

Does this then mean that the disembodied person cannot perceive? Not necessarily. What does follow from this is that if there are to be any acts of perception by the disembodied soul, they will have to be extra-sensory perceptual acts. Perception will thus involve either the addition of new and different perceptual powers, or, if we already possess such extra-sensory powers, the extension or liberation of presently abnormal or unrecognized and little used perceptual powers, such as clairvoyance and telepathy.

Similarly with *agency*. If the disembodied individual is to be able to affect a physical world, it cannot be by ordinary physical means. It does not make sense to say that a disembodied individual can type this page or move this chair in the way in which I am now doing it. If sense is to be made of the disembodied affecting the physical, extra-ordinary or para-normal powers must be attributed to it. By merely thinking or concentrating on the act and desiring it to occur, it must be able to perform it. Or better, by mere thought and desire it must be able to cause a certain effect to occur.

This kind of activity is not entirely unknown in our present world. The power of levitation has ancient claims. Recent experimenters have documented cases of individuals bending ordinary table forks and moving various objects across a table merely by thinking about it. More commonly, we sometimes feel that we can affect such things as the rolling of dice or the flight of a basketball by merely concentrating on what we want to happen.

The point to be made here is that disembodied perception and agency are not possible in the normal or ordinary sense, which is the embodied sense. If they are to be possible, we must appeal either to new powers which are conferred on the disembodied individual or, more likely, to extensions of powers which are infrequently manifested here and now. In perception, it would be to such extra-sensory abilities as telepathy and clairvoyance. For acts of agency, it must be to a "mind force," commonly termed psychokinesis.

If these abilities are real abilities and can be ascribed to a disembodied soul, it would then be possible to preserve a meaningful sense of "perceiving the world" (being affected by the world) and "acting on the world" (affecting the world). Much of our common language about perception and action would have to be deleted or replaced with the largely unfamiliar language of para-psychology. But insofar as para-psychology can develop a meaningful language describing the disembodied acquisition of information concerning the world, the communication with others who are not in physical contact with us or in our presence, and the alteration of the physical by non-physical causes, one can meaningfully say that the disembodied individual can both perceive and act.

The possibility that the disembodied individual can be an agent in the world raises a further question: What is the disembodied individual's spatial relation to the physical world? The question of spatial relations is a difficult one. On the one hand, as we argued in chapter six, to use spatial language with respect to that which is non-physical is to commit a category mistake, for spatial terms are used in their ordinary sense in reference to physical objects. Thus, for example, it does not make sense to say that my mind is in my pineal gland or in the left part of the cerebral cortex, or that my thought of a piece of cake is two inches behind my right eye or next to the thought of a warm, spring day.

On the other hand, when speaking about spiritual substances, the dualist frequently does use location terms, and he uses them in a way which he apparently takes to be meaningful. It is affirmed that John's soul is in his body and not in Mary's. It is in Minneapolis and not in St. Paul, on earth and not on any extra-terrestrial body. The latter two statements seem to follow from the first, in that it is because his soul is in his body and his body is in Minneapolis and not in St. Paul, on earth and not on the moon, that his soul is on earth in Minneapolis. In these cases location would be predicated of souls derivatively in terms of the location of the body. But this is generally not held to be the case with respect to the first statement. The soul is not in the body because it is in the head or heart or pineal gland. Rather, here we have a basic location statement which is taken by the dualist to be meaningful: the soul is located in the body. Even if some dualist wishes to claim that the soul is in the body because it is in the head or heart, we would either have to take this as a basic location

167

statement, or else eventually come to some basic statement where the soul would be located in a physical object not in virtue of being located in another physical object. But how can the dualist make such a location statement? How can he locate that which is non-physical and lacks any dimensions?

One possible way out of this puzzle is suggested (but apparently not applied to this issue) by Descartes. He distinguishes between the terms "place" and "space."

> The terms place and space are however different, because place indicates situation more expressly than magnitude or figure; while, on the contrary, we more often think of the latter when we speak of space. . . . And hence if we say that a thing is in a particular place, we simply mean that it is situated in a certain manner in reference to certain other things; and when we add that it occupies a certain space or place, we likewise mean that it is of a definite magnitude or figure.[2]

Utilizing this distinction, we might say that though a soul does not occupy a place or space (since it has no spatial magnitude), it is in a particular place in that it is situated in a certain respect to a physical body.

But what is that "certain manner" with respect to which it is situated? Clearly it cannot be spatial, though Descartes's discussion of the pineal gland makes it appear that way. Aquinas suggests that the "certain manner" is a manner of essence and function.[3] The soul is in the body *in toto* in terms of its total essence and function; it is in various parts of the body, for example, the senses, in terms of their particular functions. In this way we can locate a non-spatial entity in terms of the manifestation of its powers and its activity, while not having to do so in spatial terms involving magnitude and dimension.[4]

Applying this to our original question, we can say that the question as posed is meaningless, for we cannot use spatial location language to relate that which is non-physical to that which is physical. Any such attempt is nonsense.[5] However, if we rephrase the question, "What is its location in relation to the physical world?" we can say that the soul is located at that place where it manifests its powers and activity.

The Afterlife as an Image World

Throughout the discussion to this point we have tacitly presupposed that there is reason to think that the disembodied individual or soul would be interested in the physical world and could be involved in it in some para-normal fashion. But why should it be interested? Is there anything of significance for it in that world? And what if there are no such para-normal powers and abilities? Can anything then be said about its afterlife?

A different and most intriguing account of disembodied existence has been offered by H.H. Price. Price suggests that the Next World is a world strictly of mental images. In it we would be actively engaged in producing mental images, about which we would have desires and emotions. Though we would be cut off from any supply of sensory material, we might be able to draw upon our memory of our previous physical world to create an entire world of images. "There might be a set of visual images related to each other perspectively, with front views and side views and back views all fitting neatly together in the way that ordinary visual appearances do now."[6] Such a group of images might also contain tactual, taste, auditory, and olfactory images as well. A nexus of inter-related images would then constitute an object, which would serve as a substitute for the material objects which we perceive in this present life. The entire environment of the disembodied individual would be composed of such families of mental images, and this would serve as his world.

One might even have a visual image of the body which one had in the former life. This body image might form the center or nucleus of one's image world, such that every other image would be seen in relation to it. In this way, one might even conceive of oneself as embodied. Of course to do so would be to be mistaken. However, it would be a mistake that would be discoverable and corrigible, for this image body would be governed by a set of causal laws quite different from those which were recalled to have governed the original physical body. For example, one's wishes would be immediately fulfilled in terms of the appropriate mental images. Whereas it would take several hours for me to get to Vienna physically, I could image myself there immediately simply by wishing to be there (provided I could recall appropriate images of Vienna).

Would we not then exist in a world of deception, simply and solely created by us? As Price correctly notes, the difference between real and unreal is relative. To be real something does not have to be physical. Images themselves are real. To call something unreal is simply to say that it is different from something else with which it might be mistakenly identified. . . . An image-world, then, is only "unreal" in the sense that it is not really physical, though it might be mistakenly thought to be physical by some of those who experience it. But this only amounts to saying that the world I am describing would be an *other* world, other than this present physical world, which is just what it ought to be . . . and yet sufficiently like it to be possibly confused with it.[7]

If the individual took this image world to be a physical world, then he would be deceived. However, insofar as he understood it to be what it truly is, an image world, it would not be a world of deception, but a different, imaginal world. It would be the only world that the disembodied individual would know, and hence he could designate it as the *real* world, though in doing so he must not think that he is acquainted with anything other than what is the product of dreaming, hallucinating, imagining, and remembering. On this score it is easy to be misled by talk about a world of images and their reality. "There can be nothing more to the suggestion that the world of images is for our survivors the *real* world than the claim that imagining or dreaming or hallucinating is, in default of there being objects in an environment to perceive, all that these survivors can do."[8]

One might also wonder, if the contents of this world are determined solely by one's memories and desires, would it not be a most restricted world? One could image only what one paid attention to in the pre-mortem experience and could now recall. Novel combinations of this information could be made, but no new input gathered. In order to expand the world of the disembodied, Price has to appeal to para-normal powers. He suggests that the disembodied individual's knowledge could be increased by means of images received in telepathic communication with other disembodied souls. In this way information could be acquired about others and about what they know and remember. Indeed, he suggests that if telepathy can consist of images, one might even be able to "meet others" by having a telepathic image of their previous body. If one allows this sort of communication, and adds to it communication of some sort with an omniscient God, be it by telepathy or the beatific vision, one's range for acquiring new knowledge would become unlimited.

In this way Price's model provides a way of meaningfully speaking about an afterlife for the disembodied soul. The individual can construct an image world in which he can live. If it be a solipsistic world, the prospects might not be greatly enticing; however, if one's horizon could be expanded by extra-sensory communication with others, it might constitute a most challenging and creative environment.

Life After Death for the Embodied Individual

For those who maintain that the individual is re-created embodied in the Next Life, the problems of meaningful predication noted above do not arise. As embodied, he is in possession of all of his sense organs and hence able to sense and know the world in the same fashion as we do presently. Likewise, he can act as an agent in that world, affecting physical objects in the same manner as prior to his death.

The problems that arise for this position stem from special qualifications which are sometimes placed upon the re-creation in the Next Life. In particular, I want to mention two of them. First, there is the suggestion, originally made by St. Paul, that the re-created body is not a physical body, but a spiritual body. Unfortunately, what is meant by this is not fully spelled out, either by commentators upon Paul or by Paul himself. Some commentators suggest that "spiritual body" means that the re-created body will be composed of material other than physical matter. Others suggest it means that the body will be endowed with certain additional powers. They cite as examples the post-resurrection ability of Jesus to penetrate solid objects such as walls and to appear and disappear at will. Others contend that it simply means that the re-created body will not be of the identical physical elements which composed the original body. Still others argue that it refers to the individual whose existence has been transformed or made authentic by the Spirit.

In the passage in which he introduces the concept, St. Paul speaks mostly in terms of analogies. In response to the question of the nature of this re-created body, he introduces the analogies of the kernel of grain, the different kinds of bodies possessed by various creatures, and the difference between terrestrial and celestial bodies. The point of each of these is to stress that the re-created body will be different from the body we presently have. But the manner of difference is left unstated, and can only be guessed at from the analogies. The kernel analogy suggests that this difference is controlled by an identity of type. That is, as the corn kernel yields the corn plant, so the re-created human body will still be a human body, but of a struc-

171

ture determined by God's choice. The analogy of men, animals, birds, and fish suggests that it is not the composition of the re-created body which will be different, for the composition of men, animals, birds, and fish as material or physical flesh is the same. What differs is the proportions of the elements and the configurations involved, and the powers and abilities which result from this. This leaves open the possibility that the spiritual body might indeed be physical, but with different proportions of elements and new powers and abilities. The third analogy comparing terrestrial and astronomical bodies deals with the value placed on the body, and not with its nature. What little he does say apart from these analogies affirms that it will be an incorruptible body created by God.

In short, Paul's account of the spiritual body is generally too vague to provide us with a definite account of the nature of the re-created body or to enable us to describe the Next Life. What can be said, however, is that if the re-created body is to be changed, it cannot be changed in ways which would make it non-human or which would destroy the personal identity of the re-created individual. The parameters of personal identity and humanity would seem to constitute the only limitations to the changes which might be suggested by the phrase "spiritual body."

The second suggestion is made by John Hick. According to him, the re-created individual "is located in a resurrection world which does not stand in any spatial relationship with the physical world."[9] He suggests two reasons for this. First, he interprets "spiritual body" as meaning that the re-created individual possesses no physical properties, that he is reconstructed out of entirely different material. If this is a proper reading of "spiritual body," then clearly this body cannot be spatially related to this world. However, I see no reason for opting for this particular interpretation. At least Paul's usage of "spiritual body," as we have just pointed out, does not require any such interpretation. Secondly, Hick believes that the re-creation act will occur immediately upon death. If this were so, and if the re-created existed in a location spatially related to earth, there would exist the possibility of radio communication or rocket travel between earth and heaven. But this, he thinks, is absurd. However, as we noted in chapter four, the Biblical view is that re-creation will be in the future. For example, St. Paul felt it necessary to comfort the Thessalonians (I Thess. 4:13-18) with reassurances concerning what had not yet happened but would happen in the future to their deceased friends. Furthermore, even if re-creation were immediate, I see no objection against the possibility of radio communication with the deceased, or with the possibility of rocket travel to a heaven located on another planet or even in another galaxy (supposing heaven to be located there). The rejection of these seems to be little more than aesthetic prejudices which are emotional hangovers from the bitter campaign against the "three storied universe."

*   *   *

Our discussion has painted only a few broad strokes of the total picture of the Next Life; a host of intriguing questions remains. For one thing, what kind of social relationships will obtain in this state? Jesus stated that in the Next Life people "will not marry nor be given in marriage" (Mt. 22:30). Does this statement rule out the marital relationship, or rather does it suggest in its context that this social relation will not be for the purpose of procreation? Will the society look like H.G. Wells's futuristic society in *The Time Machine,* where everything is provided for the inhabitants without their labor or toil? But is a life without employment or occupation, production or creativity, the challenge of success or the agony of defeat, a meaningful existence?

For another thing, will the re-creation be to a perfect world or not? If so, will change be part of the Next Life, seeing that there would be no reason to change from something already perfect? But is human life meaningful without change? Since our social relationships depend upon change for their meaning and very survival, can they exist or have meaning in such a setting? Will there be any personal maturation or growth? Without the opportunity for intellectual and personal improvement, will our "humanness" be adversely affected? Popular literature frequently portrays it as a life of perpetual bliss, where the populace is passively seated by streams of clear water or perpetually strolling down golden streets. Can we recognize and appreciate endless bliss without knowing something with which to compare it? Are not boredom and suffering, meaninglessness and despair, relative?

On the other hand, if the Next Life is not a perfect world, will evil again be possible? Will we again have the opportunity to actualize our freedom in the assertion of our independence? If sin is possible, in what sense would it then be an improvement on this present life?

Other questions might be posed about the eco-structure of this world. If everyone or great numbers of people are re-created simultaneously, not to die again, will there be over-population and accompanying ecological problems? Will birth and death be permanently absent features of this world? What then of other creatures in our environment? Again these questions raise the very real issue of whether an entirely different eco-structure will affect our "humanity."

Will the Next Life be entirely different, so as to create culture shock, if not for everyone, at least for those dead for centuries or millennia? Or do not our projections for this world begin to look much like the old life? Our friends are there with their bodies, their familiar characteristics, their customary habits; similar social relationships and eco-structures obtain. There is a familiar environment, cities with places of worship, streets, and all the trappings of civilization. But if it is so much the same, does not the magic and attractiveness of immortality vanish? Do we really want to reduplicate our environment and social structure? If not, what new is to be added; what will be changed? Perhaps it is the creative possibility of the new, unknown and yet magnetic, uncertain and yet promising, which draws men to desire the experience of the Phoenix: to die and yet to live again.

NOTES

1. Terence Penelhum, *Survival and Disembodied Existence* (London: Routledge & Kegan Paul, 1970), p. 24.

2. René Descartes, *Principles of Philosophy*, Part II, Prin. XIV; in *Philosophical Works of Descartes*, I, ed. Haldane and Ross (N.Y.: Dover Publications, 1931), 261.

3. Thomas Aquinas, *Summa Theologica*, I, Q. 76, A. 8.

4. *Ibid.*, Q. 52, A. 1.

5. For example, if the statement in Revelation 6:9 be taken to give the spatial location of souls — under the physical altar — then it is nonsense. However, it can make sense if it be understood as giving the location of their particular activity, that is, their plea for vindication.

6. H.H. Price, "Survival and the Idea of 'Another World,' " *Proceedings of the Society for Psychical Research*, L, Part 182 (Jan. 1953); reprinted in

Immortality, ed. Terence Penelhum (Belmont, Cal.: Wadsworth, 1973), pp. 25-26.

7. *Ibid.*, pp. 35-36.

8. Penelhum, *op. cit.*, p. 49.

9. John Hick, *Faith and Knowledge* (Ithaca, N.Y.: Cornell University Press, 1966), pp. 183-184. Interested readers may want to consult Hick's *Death and Eternal Life* (Harper and Row), which appeared too late to be discussed in the present study.

Resurrection of the Body and Interim Existence in the New Testament

QUESTIONS HAVE BEEN RAISED WHETHER THE MONISTIC VIEW of man and, more specifically, its implications for life after death are consistent with the teachings of the New Testament. Does not the New Testament support the statement of the Apostles' Creed: I believe in the resurrection of the flesh (body) (alone)? Does not the New Testament teach that there is an interim existence (and hence an existent) between one's death and his resurrection — a tenet which we have seen is closely linked to the dualistic view of man and its associated belief in life after death? To the contrary, I wish to suggest that these two positions are not only not supported by Scripture, but are indeed at odds with it. I intend to show that according to the New Testament, resurrection (re-creation) is of persons, not of bodies alone, and that it sees no existent in objective time between one's death and his re-creation.

The Resurrection of Persons[1]

If we work *strictly* with the New Testament notion of flesh (σάρξ), two points must be noted. First, the phrase "resurrection of the flesh (σάρξ)" is not found in the New Testament at all. Secondly, the New Testament opposes any conception of the resurrection of σάρξ, as it understands the term.

"Σάρξ" has several meanings in the New Testament. It can refer to the physical or corporeal aspect of man and thus function as a synonym for "body" (Lk. 24:39; Acts 2:31; II Cor. 7:5; 12:7; Gal. 4:13).[2] It can also refer, in a somewhat ethically neutral sense, to the earthly sphere of man's existence, to the external, temporal, and visible. For example, it is used to refer to human and physical kinship relations (Rom. 1:3; 4:1; 9:3, 5, 8; I Cor. 10:18; Phm. 16), or to the realm of worldly human wisdom which only takes account of temporal or earthly features (II Cor. 1:17; Mt. 16:17). However, even in this apparently neutral sense there is an implicit antithesis established between the earthly sphere, where man leads his life paying attention to human and earthly concerns, and another dimension of life, where the focus is on the things of God.[3] This implicit antithesis leads to a third or ethical sense of σάρξ. Here σάρξ is viewed negatively insofar as one trusts solely in earthly relationships for salvation (Rom. 2:28), insofar as human wisdom views the preaching of the cross as foolishness and consequently opposes the Gospel (I Cor. 1:18f, 26), or insofar as the limitations of and confidence in the flesh provide opportunity for sin to gain control over our lives (Rom. 7:5; 8:6f). Though σάρξ itself is not viewed as inherently sinful, yet through its weakness it is open to becoming the sphere of action which leads to immorality, idolatry, anger, dissension, and so on (Gal. 5:19f).

Paul contrasts it with a life which is lived according to the promise (Gal. 4:23) or according to or by the Spirit (Rom. 8:5ff; Gal. 5:18). Σάρξ is the realm where sin is at work and which, to yield to it, results in death. To have one's life directed by it is to be hostile to God, for one is obedient to one's own evil desires and passions rather than to the commandments of God. As such, σάρξ cannot be included in the sphere of salvation. Rather, it is to be left behind, crucified (Gal. 5:24). We are to walk by the Spirit, who gives life now and who will bring us to life after death. Thus, salvation comes only through that which contrasts with σάρξ, the sphere of the Spirit.

As such, σάρξ cannot have a place in the resurrection. This is made clear by Paul in I Cor. 15:50, where he writes that flesh and blood[4] cannot inherit the kingdom. Paul's point here seems to be that that which leads to death cannot be part of the new life where death has been conquered; the corruptible and mortal can have no place in the incorruptible and immortal. The resurrection will be to a new creation, where the glorified, changed person will be controlled by the Spirit. Thus understood, the notion of the "resurrection of the flesh" is quite alien to the New Testament scheme of things.

However, as we noted above, "σάρξ" can also be understood in the sense of "body." Indeed, English translations of the Apostles' Creed usually use the phrase "the resurrection of the body."[5] Accordingly, we can ask whether the New Testament teaches the resurrection of the body (or, more precisely, the resurrection of the body alone).

Unfortunately, this formulation is likewise inadequate, again for two reasons. First, the New Testament (with one exception noted below) never uses the phrase "resurrection of the body." Rather, it speaks about the resurrection of the whole person or, better, the individual. It is just and unjust people (Lk. 14:14; Acts 24:15), Lazarus (Jn. 11:23, 24; 12:1, 9, 17), the daughter of Jairus (Mk. 5:22ff), Tabitha (Acts 9:36f), John the Baptist (Mt. 14:2ff), Jesus Christ and, indeed, anyone (any individual — Lk. 16:31; Jn. 6:39, 40, 44, 54) that is raised. Note that in all these cases it is not the body which is spoken of as being raised, but the entire person.

The other New Testament passages which directly treat the resurrection, particularly insofar as they use verb or noun forms of ἀνίστημι or ἐγείρω, either speak about the dead being raised (Mt. 10:8; 11:5ff; Mk. 12:26; Acts 26:8; I Cor. 15:16, 29, 35, 52; I Thess. 4:16; Heb. 11:35; Rev. 20:5, 6) or the resurrection of or from the dead (νεκρῶν, with or without ἐκ — Mt. 22:31; Mk. 12:25ff; Acts 4:2; 17:31-32; 23:6; 24:21; 26:23; Rom. 1:4; I Cor. 15:12, 13, 21, 42; Heb. 6:2). Again, in each of these passages what is spoken of is not dead bodies per se, but *the* dead: the dead person is, was, or will be raised.

The one exception noted above is found in Mt. 27:52-53. This is a difficult story whose genuineness has been seriously questioned. However, it would be too easy simply to dispose of this troublesome passage in this manner. Two things must be noted about the account it presents of the raising of many bodies (πολλὰ σώματα ... ἠγέρθησαν). First, the emphasis in these verses is on the *appearances* of the deceased saints ("they appeared to many"). It would seem that the reported phenomena were visual appearances, not personal encounters. As such, it would be natural to speak of the resurrection of that element or aspect which gives the appearance — the body. Secondly, the use of σῶμα here is not in contradistinction to other parts of man, that is, the soul, but rather denotes the corpses which appeared. Thus, there are no grounds in this passage for asserting that the resurrection was of the body alone, in contrast to a soul which had continued to exist.

Two other passages must be considered with regard to my contention that the New Testament does not speak of a resurrection of a body only. The first is Rom. 8:11, 23. In the context here Paul provides a contrast between the two spheres we have already discussed: that of the flesh and that of the Spirit. To attend to the former is to be hostile to God and results in sin and ultimately death (6,7). However, those in Christ Jesus are freed from their concern with the realm of earthly things, to direct their attention to the new order of the things of the Spirit (2,5). Thus, though our body, which feels the full effect of sin, suffers its consequence, namely, death (10), yet Christ Jesus will also effect the redemption of that most affected by sin (23; cf. Rom. 6:12) and give it life through the Spirit who is already working in us (11).[6] The emphasis on giving life to our bodies, then, is not that these alone will be resurrected,[7] but rather that that which felt the full effect of sin is such as to be created anew in the resurrection in a form (redemption) in which this power of the flesh (sin) will not have dominion. What is in view here by the phrase "give life to your mortal body also" must be seen in light of the contrast developed. Whereas sin has the power of death over the body, the Spirit, which had power to raise Jesus, has the power of life to restore the body and redeem it from sin's domination.

The second passage is Phil. 3:21, which states that Jesus Christ "will change our lowly body to be like his glorious body, by the power which enables him even to subject all things to himself." The context of this passage is similar to the Romans passage just discussed. Paul is contrasting the sphere of earthly concerns, where one puts one's trust in the physical act of circumcision (σάρξ) and the covenant-community consequences of it, with the sphere of the Spirit, which transcends any confidence in the flesh (2f). One's own righteousness counts as nothing in the sphere of faith (9). The enemies of the cross are those whose ultimate concern is the earthly sphere, whereas the true concern ("commonwealth") of the Christian is the heavenly sphere (18-20). With this context, it can be seen that the theme of v. 21 is not so much the resurrection, as the culmination of the trans formation from concern with and confidence in the earthly sphere to attainment of the heavenly. The culmination is the resurrection of the person (10-11), which will involve a transformation of his body to be remade like the glory-body of Jesus Christ. The passage is therefore not focusing on the resurrection of the body per se, but rather on its transformation, which will continue or complete the perfecting pro-cess already begun (12).

We may conclude from this analysis that the notion of a resurrection of only a body is a conception foreign to the New Testament.

The New Testament View of Man

A monistic anthropology also has the general support of both the Old Testament and the New. In the Old Testament Hebraic perspective man is a whole or unity. Though various aspects of man are mentioned (soul, spirit, breath, heart, bowels), they are not different elements of man capable of separate existence, but constitute different aspects of the total person. Though the New Testament writers do use the Greek term ψυχή (soul), not only is its usage rare, but with the exception of Mt. 6:25-26, 10:28, and I Thess. 5:23,[8] "ψυχή" is not a complementary term to "σῶμα." Rather, it refers to the natural physical life (Mt. 6:28; Acts 20:10); to the true life as distinguished from mere physical life (Mk. 8:35); to the whole person (Mt. 11:29; Acts 2:41; 7:14; 27:37; Rom. 2:9; 13:1); or to the inner man as the place of decision (Jn. 10:24; Acts 14:2; 15:24; Col. 3:23; Eph. 6:6) or of experiences of joy, sorrow, love, and so on (Mt. 12:18; Mk. 14:34; Lk. 12:19).[9]

Indeed, the infrequency with which Paul uses "soul" (13 times) is noteworthy, suggesting the relative unimportance of the soul-concept for him. It is true that Paul's anthropology might not be as clearly and uniformly monistic as generally thought. The analogy of the tent in II Cor. 5:1-10[10] is disconcertingly dualistic, as is I Cor. 7:34. However, not only are these exceptions to Paul's general train of thought, but they can best be explained, not on the grounds that he is dualistically inclined, but on the grounds that his anthropology is not developed philosophically. His concern was not to present a coherent anthropology in consonance with or contrast to Hellenistic thought, but to develop a theology in relation to the redemption of man. Despite a few exceptions, then, Pauline anthropology, and New Testament anthropology in general, is monistic.

As such, the New Testament writers would not be concerned with the resurrection merely of the body, so that it may be subsequently conjoined to a continuously existing soul. Rather, they are concerned with the resurrection of the whole person from the dead. Of course this will involve the body; life after death is an embodied existence. The question "How are the dead raised?" leads to the query "With what kind of body do they come?" (I Cor. 15:35). But the resurrection does not *merely* involve the body. There is no continuously existing inner self or soul; the entire resurrection is a creative act of God.

Resurrection as Re-creation

Since the New Testament emphasis is not on a continuing soul which is to be reunited with a resurrected body, but is rather on the creative act by which God brings the whole person again to life, it might be appropriate to replace the term resurrection with the more suitable term, re-creation.

The language of resurrection is misleading when it suggests that the very thing which died will be raised again. Not only would this seem generally contrary to any factual possibility, given the disintegration of bodies upon death and the dispersal of their constituent elements, but it fails to appreciate the New Testament view that resurrection is an historical, eschatological event which involves more than a mere raising of the deceased to live again. The resurrected acquires a new mode of existence. Paul speaks of the resurrected body as a changed body. Whereas it died in weakness and dishonor, as a physical body modelled after the image of Adam who was made from dust, so the new body will be raised in power and glory to be an imperishable, immortal, spiritual body (I Cor. 15:35-53). Paul does not describe this body in detail. Rather, he stresses two things: that it will be changed,[11] and that the model for the changes is the resurrected body of the man from heaven, Jesus Christ (I Cor. 15:49; Phil. 3:21).

Indeed, since "re-creation" is much more in line with the New Testament view of the order of things, one might wonder why the New Testament writers preferred to use the term "resurrection" rather than "re-creation." Part of the answer might lie in their reservation of the concept of re-creation to the spiritual regeneration produced by the salvific work of Christ. The regenerated person is a new man (Eph. 2:15; 4:24); a new creation (II Cor. 5:17; Gal. 6:15), possessing a new nature (Col. 3:10), who has experienced a new birth (John 3:3ff). Thus, in the order of creation, the future resurrection was only a further work in the re-creative process wrought on man, begun by the work of Christ now. It would appear

181

far too narrow to these authors to restrict "re-creation" to the eschatological work of bringing the dead to life.

Whatever the reason, it would seem more appropriate today to speak of the re-creation of the person subsequent to his death as being the Biblical view. This would avoid any necessity to explain why our future life is not really a resurrection of the same body, which has long since disappeared, and would open the door to see our future re-creation as a part of, as one stage in, God's total creative process.

The Problem of the Interim

According to the New Testament, God's re-creative work with respect to our post-mortem existence is still future. The Day of the Lord (II Thess. 2:2), the parousia (I John 3:2), the End (I Cor. 15:24) has not yet occurred. Paul instructs the Thessalonians that the second coming of the Lord and the accompanying re-creation is still future. As such the re-creation of the dead remains both a hope and a Christian comfort.

That the re-creation is future raises the question whether there is an interim state of human or personal existence between the time of one's death and the time of one's re-creation. If it is the case that man is to be considered as a unified being along monistic lines of thought and not as an embodied soul, and if the divine re-creation of man is still future, it would seem to follow that the individual human person does not exist during this interim. He ceases to exist at his death, and begins again to exist at his re-creation.

Unfortunately, when theologians who adopt a monistic position reach this point, they frequently fail to carry through consistently the ideas for which they argued. As a case in point, I refer to Oscar Cullmann, who in his well-known little book, *The Immortality of the Soul or the Resurrection of the Dead?*, reaches conclusions similar to those we have come to above, though by means of quite different arguments. However, after arriving at an apparently monistic view of man, who is to be resurrected in the End, Cullmann promptly proceeds to betray the very cause for which he has argued, for he turns to a discussion of the state of the person in the interim between death and re-creation. Cullmann argues, on the basis of three passages — Lk. 23:42; 16:22f; and Phil. 1:23 — that the individual human person continues to exist in the interim. "The dead in Christ share in the tension of the interim time. But this means not *only* that they are waiting. It means that for them, too, something decisive happened with Jesus' death and Resurrection."[12]

And what is the state of man in the interim time? Cullmann continues, "It is precisely those images used in the New Testament to describe the condition of the dead in Christ which prove that even now, in this interim state of the dead, the Resurrection of Christ — the anticipation of the End — is already effective. They are 'with Christ'."[13]

The dead, though without a body, are only sleeping; they are not non-existent. This state of nakedness is not the natural state, but one which is made possible by the divine intervention of the Holy Spirit, and it will be rectified at the resurrection. In the meantime the inner man (soul) continues to exist, having been renewed by the Holy Spirit, the power of life, who is in us.

But does not this analysis destroy the very position for which we have argued? On the one hand, it breaks up the unity of man and throws us back into the Greek dualistic view of man which we (and Cullmann) have contended is contrary to the New Testament. For now Cullmann is arguing for the actuality that the person of man (the soul) continues to exist disembodied by the power of the Holy Spirit during the interim time. It can only do so if it is an entity capable of an existence independent of the body.

It is true that this position differs from the Greek position in that the soul is not inherently immortal; Cullmann affirms that its immortality is made possible only by the work of the Spirit. Yet in arguing that an essential part of man can continue to exist subsequent to death he is in effect adopting a Greek dualistic position: man consists of two elements, one of which is capable of existing independently of the other.

On the other hand, the concept of the resurrection (of the person) from the dead, which we have seen to be the Scriptural position, must now be replaced with the resurrection of the body alone, which we have seen is foreign to the New Testament. For if the inner man (the soul) exists in the interim, it need not be resurrected or re-created, but only awakened and conjoined to a re-created body. We can no longer speak of the re-creation of the individual person, but only of the re-creation of the body.[14]

But what of Cullmann's argument for his position? Cullmann supports his view from the three passages noted above. I first want to look at these passages to see whether they indeed support Cullmann, and then analyze one other passage to which appeal is sometimes made to show an interim existence of man between his death and re-creation.

Cullmann appeals to the parable of Lazarus and the rich man (Lk. 16:19ff) to show that there is an existent in the interim. As he rightly notes, this passage does not speak of the End time and the resurrection of the body, but apparently about the present age. However, despite this, the parable provides no grounds for a theology of interim existence. For one thing, it is notoriously impossible to ground a theological doctrine on a parable. The purpose of parables was not to construct or illustrate theological theories. Secondly, the presence of the parable among the teachings of Jesus does not necessarily mean that his approval is being given, either by himself or by Luke, to the anthropological ideas contained therein. As has been frequently pointed out, it is very likely that Jesus was adapting a story popular among the Jews to his own purposes. Hugo Gressman adduces parallels from Egyptian and Rabbinic sources.[15] In the Egyptian account a rich man, clothed in his finery and accompanied by many attendants, is carried to his burial, while at the same time a poor man covered only by a mat is buried without attendants. The observer thinks that the rich man is favored, until given the opportunity to journey to the underworld, where he sees that there the men's earthly roles are reversed. A version of the same story, he argues, was present in Palestine in the time of Jesus. If this is the case, then it would seem that, rather than advocating the theological/anthropological motifs contained therein and an interim existence, Jesus was utilizing and adapting a common story to make his point about compensation for conditions experienced in this life and that a miraculous appearance of one raised from the dead would not convince those not converted by Moses and the prophets.

Cullmann's two other passages are Phil. 1:23, where Paul states that it is better to be "with Christ" than to continue living on earth, and Lk. 23:43, where the repentent thief is promised immediate conveyance to Paradise with Jesus. Whereas Cullmann sees these passages as showing that in their expression of a special proximity of the dead to Christ the New Testament affirms an interim existence for the dead, I believe another and more consistent explanation can be given.

The view one takes of these passages depends ultimately upon the view of time which one thinks is being expressed here. As noted in chapter five, time can be considered objectively (In exactly five minutes the rocket will be launched) or subjectively in terms of our experience of time (Time goes fast when you are having fun). Which view of time is to be found in these two passages? The clue is given by Cullmann, though he fails to see the significance of it: the passages teach the *experienced* immediacy of being "with Christ." They are not speaking about objective time, but rather subjective time. Though the time between death and resurrection at the End is objectively long, subjectively it is experienced as immediate. The reason for this is that in the interim there is no consciousness, for there is no individual to be conscious. And without consciousness, there can be no awareness of passing time. Thus Paul can say that to die is to be with (to experience) Christ (at the next conscious moment).

This is not a case of soul-sleep, as suggested by Cullmann. There is no soul to sleep. When the New Testament refers to the dead as sleeping, it is not making an ontological claim about their condition or status.[16] Rather, it is a metaphorically nice way of speaking about the dead (Jn. 11:11; I Cor. 7:39; 15:20, 51; I Thess. 4:13, 14).[17]

But more important than the niceties of language, it strongly suggests that death is not the end of human existence. Just as a person who is sleeping can be raised, so too the dead, as "sleeping," have the possibility of being re-created and living again. This is perhaps the significance of the difficult account in Mt. 9:24ff where Jesus says that the girl is not dead, but only sleeping. People who considered her as dead had no hope for her. But because Jesus considered her as sleeping, he saw that there was hope indeed that she could be resurrected to live again. He saw a potentiality in her that the others, unaware of the power of God, could not see. The metaphor "sleep," then, does not describe the ontological state of the dead, but rather refers to the possibilities of the deceased: that though they now no longer exist, by the power of God they can be re-created to live again.

One other passage, not referred to by Cullmann, should be mentioned. In Rev. 6:9 John records the vision of the opening of the six seals. When the fifth seal was opened, he saw "under the altar the souls of those who had been slain for the word of God and for the witness they had borne." Lest one fall prey to the temptation of taking this passage as teaching about the ontological interim-state of the deceased, it must be emphasized first that the entire context of the book is one of symbolism, imagery, allegory, and metaphor. Thus one is treading upon dangerous waters if one takes this literally (unsymbolically) as a teaching about the existence of disembodied souls during the interim. Rather, the symbolism of the souls under the altar stresses that martyrdom on earth for the cause of Christ is considered ultimately a sacrifice to God,[18] whereas the white robe given to them (11) stresses that their righteousness will not be forgotten in the re-creation (Rev. 3:1-5).

Secondly, it should be noted that the souls here mentioned are hardly disembodied. They are in a position (albeit metaphorically) under the altar, they cry out for vengeance, and they are clothed in white robes and told to continue resting. All these are physical activities, hardly characteristic of disembodied souls.

Indeed, the other uses of ψυχή in Revelation give no indication that such a disembodied state is in view or even possible. ψυχή is used to refer either to the physical life of things (8:9; 16:3 — animals; 12:11 — martyrs), or to the person as a whole (18:13; 20:4[19]). Thus it would be difficult indeed to treat the symbolic vision of John as grounds for any New Testament belief in the existence of a disembodied person in an interim state between death and re-creation.

Conclusion

In conclusion, we have seen that there is no New Testament warrant for speaking about the resurrection of the body apart from the total re-creation of the individual person. The re-creation of the body will be only one aspect of the total re-creative process: the re-creation of the individual human person. Further, we have seen that there is no New Testament warrant for holding that there is an interim existence between death and re-creation. Death brings the non-existence of the individual in objective time. Thus, in place of the commonly repeated affirmation of the Apostles' Creed that we believe in the resurrection of the flesh (body) (alone), it would be more in line with New Testament teaching to speak of the

Appendix

resurrection of the dead, or even better, to speak of the re-creation of individual human persons in the future by the creative power of God.

NOTES

1. From my article, "Resurrection of the Body, Re-Creation and Interim Existence," *Journal of Theology for Southern Africa*, 20 (1977).

2. This sense of σάρξ will be considered below.

3. Rudolph Bultmann, *Theology of the New Testament*, I (London: SCM Press, 1952), 235-236.

4. Eduard Schweizer, in his article on σάρξ in *The Theological Dictionary of the New Testament*, VII, suggests that "flesh and blood" here "denotes the whole man with all his functions" (p. 129). This interpretation would seem unlikely, for then the whole individual, as a particular person, could not experience life after death. But Paul's entire argument is directed to show that this will be the case. Thus, this phrase must refer to man as seen from the perspective of his corruptibility. That is, the individual can live after death, but changes in his perishable nature must take place.

5. Latin: *carnis resurrectionem*; Greek: σαρκὸς ἀνάστασιν.

6. Part of the difficulty of this passage is how to understand πνεῦμα in v. 10. Some have argued that since πνεῦμα here seems to stand structurally opposed to the human σῶμα, the πνεῦμα is human. As such, though the body die, the spirit remains alive. This would suggest an underlying anthropological dualism. However, two things might be said against such an interpretation. First, throughout the passage, with the exception of v. 16 where the plural "our spirits" is used, πνεῦμα refers to the Spirit of God or the Spirit of Christ. Thus it would seem consistent to so interpret it in v. 10. Secondly, Paul does not assert that the spirit is alive, but that it is life (ζωή), which would constitute an unusual appellation for his view of the human spirit. V. 11 confirms that what is referred to here is the life-imparting function of the Spirit.

7. Note that in this very passage (11) it was not the body of Jesus that was raised, but Jesus Christ himself, as a person, who was raised from the dead.

8. Even these exceptional passages provide little ground for asserting anthropological dualism in the New Testament. In Mt. 6:25-26 ψυχή clearly stands for physical life viewed qualitatively, not for a separate spiritual entity. In I Thess. 5:23 the emphasis is on the whole person; the use of "body, soul, and spirit" simply serves to underscore the completeness of the whole person. Though Mt. 10:28 is the most dualistic of the three,

187

it is interesting to note that in the Lucan parallel, ψυχή is omitted completely, thus removing any hint of psycho-physical dualism.

9. See "ψυχή," *The Theological Dictionary of the New Testament*, IX, 637-656.

10. This analogy is likewise developed dualistically in II Pet. 1:13, 14.

11. Though, clearly, the change cannot be such as to affect adversely the personal identity of the deceased.

12. Oscar Cullmann, *The Immortality of the Soul or the Resurrection of the Dead?* (London: The Epworth Press, 1958), p. 51. See also W. David Stacey, *The Pauline View of Man* (London: Macmillan & Co., 1956), p. 142.

13. Cullmann, p. 52.

14. It is significant that Cullmann himself has to replace "resurrection from the dead" with "resurrection of the body" when he gets to this discussion (pp. 56f).

15. For a summary of the tales see H.M. Creed, *The Gospel According to St. Luke* (London: Macmillan & Co., 1957), pp. 208-210.

16. Cullmann, p. 51.

17. Cullmann thinks that the statement that they have or are fallen asleep indicates that the deceased are still *in time*, "otherwise the problem in I Thess. 4:13ff would have no meaning" (p. 49). However, the problem of the future existence of the presently deceased has even more significance if the deceased presently do not exist (in objective time). Thus, the question concerns their future existence and when in objective time this re-creation will occur.

18. R.H. Charles, *Revelation*, I, *The International Critical Commentary* (Edinburgh: T. & T. Clark, 1920), p. 174.

19. It should be noted with reference to this verse that the writer speaks about "souls coming to life," hardly a view which, if taken literally, would support an interim existence.

Index

189